"In *All Set Free*, Matthew Distefano articulates what an Evangelical theology might look like when shorn of it's Janus-faced deity. This is a challenging and provocative study which utilizes the mimetic theory of René Girard to reframe the perspective by which readers read the Bible. This will be the book you could put into the hands of any person seeking the post-Christian Abba of Jesus."

—**MICHAEL HARDIN**
Executive Director of Preaching Peace, editor/author of eight books, including
The Jesus Driven Life

"*All Set Free* is a fascinating integration of René Girard's mimetic theory with a biblical grounded Christian universalism. Every Sunday countless Evangelicals sing 'Come, Now is the Time to Worship.' Through a careful exposition of the relevant biblical passages, Distefano demonstrates the good news and literal truth of its chorus: 'One day every tongue will confess/One day every knee will bow...'"

—**RIC MACHUGA**
Professor of Philosophy, Butte College; Author of *Three Theological Mistakes: How to Correct Enlightenment Assumptions about God, Miracles, and Free Will*

"*All Set Free* is a splendid contribution to an ever-growing theological conversation springing from the work of René Girard, one that is liberating the Christian tradition from its deadly optics of violence in favor of something much more in character with Jesus's forgiving and loving Abba. Distefano makes the case for the reconciliation of all humanity with God, in a fluent, engaging style, rising often to eloquence, presenting multiple arguments to bring out the inconsistency in textual interpretations demanding eternal retributive punishment. Most of all, he gives us a positive message of a nonviolent God whose deep attraction promises to make the rote prayer of 'your kingdom come...on earth' become thrilling human reality. A vital book for twenty-first-century Christianity."

—**ANTHONY W. BARTLETT**
Co-Founder and Contributing Theologian at Theology and Peace; Author of *Virtually Christian: How Christ Changes Human Meaning and Makes Creation New*

"In *All Set Free*, Matthew Distefano offers his readers many gifts. For those asking new and intellectually challenging questions about God, he provides a map of the terrain, including areas which other maps cordon off with 'here there be monsters.' For those whose religious communities have ostracized them for their questions, he offers vulnerability and companionship. This is not a lawyer's brief, defending a position at all costs. Neither is it an exposé, claiming to unmask deficient theologies. Rather, it displays the gift of joy that comes with discovering the God of peace."

—**GREGORY A. CLARK**
Professor of Philosophy, North Park University

"*All Set Free* begins with the assumption that the character of God is revealed in the nonviolent story of Jesus. The result is a merciful and loving God, who would not kill many thousands of people (as is often assumed from the traditional reading of the Old Testament) and who would not condemn millions of people to fiery torture after death for unending billions of years. Instead the book argues for a 'universal reconciliation' in which punishment is not rejected but serves a purifying function so that eventually all are reconciled to God. *All Set Free* is thus a welcome addition to the growing body of literature that challenges the inherited ideas of a violent God and a God for whom forgiveness and salvation depend on a propitiating death of Jesus. The assumption that drives the book obviously requires rethinking a number of inherited doctrines and also developing a new understanding of biblical interpretation. This book pursues these questions through a lens focused by René Girard. For those who want a Girardian analysis, this is a very interesting book, which concludes with a heart-felt invitation to live peacefully by living in and imitating the peace-loving God who is revealed in Jesus."

—**J. DENNY WEAVER**
Professor Emeritus of Religion, Bluffton University

"So many of us are finding our way out of the penal atonement theory with all its prohibitions and implicit violence. In *All Set Free*, Matthew Distefano stands in this tradition and does it convincingly and with conviction. I hope many, sensing something wrong with Christianity, will read this book and be encouraged on their own journey toward a God who actually brings Good News."

—TOM TRUBY
Member of Theology & Peace; United Methodist pastor in the Oregon-Idaho Annual Conference

"In *All Set Free*, Matthew Distefano presents a way of reading the scriptures that will be new to many. And therein lies its value. We do not gain new insight by simply affirming what we already believe, we expand our thinking by exposing ourselves to ideas that might contradict our current believes. Using René Girard's anthropological insights, Distefano creates a context in which to read the scriptures that exposes the god of violence as human projection, and unveils the Father of Jesus Christ as the inversion to this human projection. A very timely book indeed."

—ANDRE RABE
Founder of Always Loved Ministries and Author of *Desire Found Me*

"In *All Set Free*, Matthew Distefano contributes an accessible yet accurate synthesis of how post-Evangelicals might integrate the discoveries of mimetic theory into an increasingly clear vision of the non-retributive God. The author heeds Michael Hardin's call to hear Jesus say, 'Be not afraid,' to its conclusions in ultimate reconciliation. Distefano shows how such a move brings personal healing to those battered by the unChristlike gods. A helpful synthesis."

—BRADLEY JERSAK
Author of *A More Christlike God*

All Set Free

All Set Free

How God is Revealed in Jesus
and Why That is Really Good News

Matthew J. Distefano
Foreword by Michael Machuga

RESOURCE *Publications* · Eugene, Oregon

ALL SET FREE
How God is Revealed in Jesus and Why That is Really Good News

Resource Publications
An Imprint of Wipf and Stock Publishers
199 W. 8th Ave., Suite 3
Eugene, OR 97401

www.wipfandstock.com

ISBN 13: 978-1-4982-3458-0

Manufactured in the U.S.A.   09/29/2015

To Lyndsay and Elyse, Michael and Speri.

Contents

Foreword

WHAT YOU BELIEVE CAN be important. If you wish to travel to Hawaii, then what you believe about geography is important. If you enjoy life, and you would like to continue living, then what you believe about gravity is of utmost importance. But when it comes to spirituality, faith is fundamentally opposed to stubborn belief. Faith, as I use the word, is the attitude that no matter what happens, God is good. A person who refuses to amend their beliefs, who thinks: "If God does not happen to work how I expect, then all is lost," has little faith in the goodness of God. Spending your life primarily working toward a correct belief in God completely misses the point anyway. True spirituality is not praying to God while going for a walk—true spirituality is simply going for a walk. True spirituality is not philosophizing about God for a further purpose—true spirituality is philosophizing simply because it is enjoyable.

Sitting by the fire-pit with Matthew—recklessly flinging ideas across the blaze—is one of my favorite things in the world. Neither is labeled a heretic or satanist, nor accused of being in a cult, which is a welcome relief considering our views. We would love to invite others to our festive gatherings but have found that most are afraid of honest discussions such as these. This is understandable as the fear that correct belief is the ticket to Heaven is a powerful trap. The fear that "you must believe in an everlasting hell in order to be saved" is the most powerful trap of all. But doesn't true love cast out fear and isn't God the very essence of love? In fact, God *is* love and it is he and only he who has the power to conquer fear. So, to reduce God's love down to some eschatological argument seems irresponsible. I submit that love can never be reduced to an argument—to words. Love is tacit and we who have experienced it have faith that in the end, all will be well.

Coming from an Arminian background, I must admit that I never experienced the fullness of love from that understanding of God. I certainly never experienced his peace. For sake of argument, let's say free will *does* exist. Does this not beg the question: "Why does God put such emphasis on it?" Does not a parent care more about the quality of existence than free will? I know of no parent with such a high regard for free will that he would let his child walk on a freeway. That is not responsible. That is not love. In fact, that does not sound like the God Matthew and I frequently talk about.

As for Calvinism: I have no long term experience with that understanding of God and I see no reason to attempt one. I see very little, if any, grace in him. It seems salvation is by a work of some sort—perhaps the work of active belief. Otherwise, by what standard are the elect chosen? Or, rather, is it because of sheer capriciousness? I am not sure which is worse.

Relax, slow down, and enjoy this book. Philosophize for the sake of philosophizing. God understands that you are fallible and that you will never completely understand him—he created you, for crying out loud! God is more concerned that you experience him. Experience his love, his beauty, and his creativity. Experience life! All are rectified already.

Michael Machuga

Preface

IN THE FALL OF 2014, I set out to write my first book. I had no idea who I was actually writing for or what exactly I was going to say. I believed that God *literally* would reconcile all in the end but was not sure exactly how I would convey that message. However, I knew *something* had to be said.

I began with only an outline, some notes, my journal, a couple books to draw from and a whole lot of desire. As the process evolved, every outline I came up with was eventually tossed out the window. My notes grew into binders full of articles, journal entries, dissertations, essays, song lyrics, and even debates. My journal became four journals. My library grew from a few handy books to shelves full of books I may never get to. And the desire to reach others burned (pardon the terrible pun) within me the entire time.

Writing this book was the greatest challenge of my life. It was a challenge due in part to the overwhelming resistance by some to the doctrine of universal reconciliation. I have been met with many false accusations—*"Satanist, false prophet, wolf in sheep's clothing!"* And I cannot recount how many times I have been told: *"You're going to hell!"* In the midst of this strong push-back from numerous Christians, I have also met so many wonderful people who have supported me through and through, who seem to be experiencing the very same push-back I am. In all, it has been worth it and will continue to be worth it; but it has not always been easy.

As far as the process of writing a book goes, I must admit that I did not expect to perform this much editing and re-writing. If only authoring a book were as easy as something like journaling! At times, it was actually something I looked forward to, but other times, it was dreadful. But now that I am finally finished, looking back, I am shocked at how quickly everything came together. All in all, it was a very gratifying experience and one which I will never forget.

This book is the culmination of a journey I began long ago, but it certainly is not the culmination of my theological pilgrimage. It is, however, the long-awaited answer to a question I set out to answer many years ago: If there is a God, *Is he/she violent?* Responding to that question took a lot of time and during some of the process, I was tormented by my non-answer. However, now that I believe I *do* have a solid answer, I am comforted by the fact that I can confidently respond, "no, God is *not* violent." My hope is that this book properly backs-up this claim. I hope it becomes more and more clear just *how* God is fully revealed, for the first time, in Jesus Christ. Never again should we be under the belief that the gods are angry, that the gods demand sacrifice, that the gods need blood. Jesus shows us all of that is false and my hope is that I fully do this theology justice.

Acknowledgments

First and foremost, I have to thank my wonderful wife, Lyndsay. She has been with me through thick and thin, good and bad, "rich" and poor. The past eleven years have been a roller coaster yet she has stuck with me through it all. Her grace and mercy so closely resembles that of Jesus and without her Christ-like spirit, I could not have written this book.

My parents, Dave and Sharon Wohnoutka, have supported me throughout my entire life. Without either, I could not be where I am at today. Although both may disagree on some matters of theology, they have supported me throughout this whole process and I am confident will continue to support my future endeavors.

I could not have kept my sanity without my dear friend Michael Machuga, who, like me, questions the status quo of institutionalized religion. Countless conversations around the bonfire on his back porch have been invaluable for me. Like they say, "the apple does not fall far from the tree" and such is the case with Mike. Having author and philosopher, Ric Machuga, as a father has been a blessing as Mike has given me more than enough to chew on throughout the years. Mike is the best *best-friend* anyone could have.

My friend Sandy Simmons devoted countless hours editing and offering feedback throughout. I am truly blessed to have a friend who is willing to help me out like that. Also, I have to mention Race MoChridhe, who professionally copy-edited my manuscript *pro bono*. His willingness to challenge my ideas and devote so many hours to this project shows his servant's heart. I am truly grateful.

I am continually amazed by how insightful my friend Michael Hardin is. His wisdom, knowledge, and passion have helped ignite this drive to bring the peace of Jesus to a hurting world. Without him, I would have never met all the wonderful people at the 2015 Making Peace Conference.

They *all* showed me what Christian community looks like. The section entitled "Personal Healing," in the concluding chapter, is for them!

I must offer a warm "thank you" to Andre and Mary-Ann Rabé—*they have a beautiful way of delivering this message of a non-violent Abba.* Oh, and anyone who buys me delicious Thai food is alright in my book!

To all my friends and family whom I do not mention by name: *Thank you.* Thank you for supporting me. Thank you for loving me. Thank you for being there for me no matter what. Thank you also to those specifically who babysit my daughter—*your kind-heartedness is evident in her imitation of you all.* This book would have never been completed had it not been for all of the help.

I must thank all of those whom I sent the manuscript to for feedback, insight, and corrections. They are too numerous to name but I am personally grateful for all of their willingness to offer their beautiful and imaginative minds to a schmuck like me.

And to the one first in my heart—this book is for Elyse. *I hope this material gives her peace when she is old enough to decipher theology for herself. The divine is nothing to fear so, in all things, have peace knowing the Father is for us all, forever and always.*

Introduction
A Brief Autobiography

IF YOU TOLD THE Matthew Distefano of five years ago, "*You are going to write a book about God,*" that person would have thought you were *insane*. However, here I am, *writing a book about God*—not thinking myself insane. Even mentioning my faith at one point in my life would not have been the easiest thing for me to do, let alone pour my thoughts onto hundreds of pages of paper. I used to struggle with how much I wanted to love God, but did so in vain. On one hand, I held Jesus of Nazareth in very high esteem, thoroughly compelled by the story of how an obscure Jewish rabbi would live a sinless and non-violent life in order to somehow save mankind (or a portion of mankind if you are a Calvinist) from their sin. On the other hand, I was a free-thinker who never wanted to be confined within the four walls of the box known as institutionalized Christianity. For me, Jesus and Christianity did not line up; they were irreconcilable.

If I am going to expect you to take seriously my arguments contained in this book, I think it is important to know where I came from. Like everyone, I too view everything through my own subjective lens, which developed because of my own particular life-events. If I remember correctly, I was baptized in a non-denominational, Protestant church when I was nine years old. However, I "gave my heart to the Lord" as early as five. Throughout my childhood, I learned biblical stories and cited Bible verses, but the only thing that stuck in my head was that, if I ceased "believing" in Jesus, *I was going to hell.* Hell was concluded as early as five—*not exactly during the age of reason.* I can recall reading the following from the book of Matthew: "But I tell you that anyone who is angry with a brother or sister will be subject to judgment. Again, anyone who says to a brother or sister, 'raca,' is answerable to the court. And anyone who says, 'You fool!' will be in danger of the fire of hell." (Matthew 5:22—NIV) To my young mind, this was psychologically devastating—so much so that I can recall having night terrors where I ran through my house screaming "snake eyes"; not aware who any of my family were. *I was convinced I was eternally damned!* Moreover, I was also well familiar with the verse that reads: "but whoever blasphemes against the Holy Spirit will never be forgiven; they are guilty of an eternal sin." (Mark 3:29—NIV) I reasoned that since "blaspheming God is *saying God's name in vain*, blaspheming the Holy Spirit must be the very same thing." It seemed like sound reasoning at the time and no adult I knew told me otherwise.[1] Christianity seemed really terrifying to me, but I "knew" walking away meant God was going to burn me with *literal flames* for all eternity.

It was not until my mid-twenties that I began to question all institutions, whether religious, political, or otherwise. My philosophy on *everything* began to change. I went from being a fairly conservative Evangelical to an in-the-closet agnostic who pretended to know the answers regarding questions of faith. However, during these years, I felt like nothing more than a fraud. I assisted in leading worship nearly every Sunday for roughly seven years, spending an estimated ten to twelve hours per week at my busiest. Yet, if anyone would have asked me *why I believe what I believe*, I could have offered no answer. I was tormented by certain doctrinal statements I was told were true, including the idea that God is violent. *It was just something I had to deal with.* Deal with it I did—I ended up walking away.

Now, years later, here I am—convinced so strongly about something that I want to "proclaim upon the rooftops[2]" what I believe is the true gospel. I hope this book can be my rooftop from where I can proclaim the truth; finding the hearts and souls of believers and non-believers alike. I am writing to Christians who have inevitably questioned the Western doctrine of hell, the faith in a violent and retributive god, and the politics of the church in the West. I am also writing to non-Christians who avoid Jesus for these very same reasons.

I truly believe God is revealed to humanity in the person of Jesus Christ, "who is the Savior of all people, especially of believers." (1 Timothy 4:10) If you are like me, you have doubted your own salvation—it is likely every Christian has at one point. However, I believe I make a strong case

---

1. For a detailed analysis of "the unpardonable sin," see Talbott, *Inescapable Love of God*, 98–101.

2. See Matthew 10:27.

that we no longer need to worry about our eternal destiny. If you adhere to the doctrine of eternal conscious torment or annihilationism, I hope this book challenges you to reevaluate those doctrines and see if they stand up to scrutiny. Years ago, I did the same thing. If you hold to the doctrine of universal reconciliation, either hopeful or convinced, I hope this book strengthens your stance and builds you up in your faith. And if you are a non-Christian, I hope it helps paint a picture of God that actually makes sense —a God that is here for the benefit of *all of humanity*. I hope and pray that I am correct in my stance because if I am, then God truly will "reconcile all things to himself."[3] What a glorious day that will be . . .

3. See Colossians 1:20.

PART I

PRESUPPOSITIONS
AND FAULTY REASONING

1

Theological Presuppositions

AN INTRODUCTION TO UNIVERSAL RECONCILIATION

I TRY TO REMIND people of the importance of defining terms before entering into a discussion or "debate" of any kind. Thus, I find it appropriate to define what I mean when I use such phrases as "universal reconciliation," "ultimate redemption," or simply, in the case of this book, "Universalism." For now, I will use a broad definition developed by nineteenth-century Universalist educator Thomas Sawyer. I feel it is a definition most, if not all, "Christian Universalists" would take no issue with. It reads: "The doctrine of universal salvation; or in other words, of the final holiness and happiness of all humans, to be effected by the grace of God, through the ministry of his son, Jesus Christ."[1] Now, if you feel the desire to throw this book down in anger and charge me with "heresy," you would most likely not be alone. Yet, it is not only my, but a growing number of others' belief that this is precisely the fate of humanity. I hope not only to present a compelling case as to why I believe what I believe, but to ease some of the rift between Christians who hold steadfast to the traditions of Calvin or Augustine and those who try to explore an alternate view. So, I kindly ask that you hold on and read further.

One need not be a scholar to understand the material presented throughout this book. It was not written by one! However, Christians are

1. Allen, "What Is 'Christian Universalism'?," para. 8.

3

meant to think, to reason, to philosophize. We are called to ask the hard questions: *Is God violent or not? Does he love everyone?* The answers seem simple to me, but others draw different conclusions. *Something's gotta give.* Luke 10:27 instructs us to, among other things, love God with our entire mind. *Metánoia*, the Greek word translated to "repent," literally means "a change of mind." Furthermore, the writer of 1 Peter tells us to "always be ready to make your defense to anyone who demands from you an accounting for the hope that is in you" (1 Peter 3:15—NRSV). In other words, we must use our minds to defend the reason for the hope within us. There is a theme here, and it is that our minds must be involved in order to know God . . . heart, soul, strength, and *mind*.

This will be a book that will challenge most Christians. It was a challenge to write! But, if I can address some of the emotional reactions that seem to bubble up at the very idea that God *may not have* designed a place where the wicked who denied *our* Savior go to burn for eternity, then maybe some *minds* will be at least open to hearing some radically "good news." I empathize with those who view my interpretation of the "good news" as an attack on the very core of what it means to be "Christian." *It does not feel good to be attacked.* Trust me, this is no such attack. It is, however, a call for others to challenge their own theologies, which can be ever-so-frightening.

Throughout my encounters with others, I have too often heard things like: *If you take away hell, you take away a fact about scripture.* Many who claim this know *nothing* about anything contrary to their own eschatological views. I will, in the sections that follow, demonstrate why this line of presuppositional thinking does not exactly lend itself to thinking outside the box. Rather, more often than not, it confines one to assume that what one is initially told in life must be true, despite all evidence contrary to that initial belief. I feel it is time for the cobwebs of presuppositional Christian thinking to be cleared away. Then, as I will argue throughout this book, the full scope of God's grace, mercy, glory, sovereignty, and love can be understood by the majority of my brethren (both current and future). Time will tell if this happens, as I can only hope Christianity is on the brink of something amazing.

WHO IS GOD?

Our view of Scripture is not as near as [sic] important as the hermeneutic we practice. When it is used to bear false witness against

God, it is its most pernicious. If Jesus reveals the character of the Creator by the choice to hear and allow his person and life to be a witness to the Creator, then it behooves us to question those elements of our faith, theory and practice that are contrary to the person and mission of Jesus.[2]

Since many of our presuppositions about life arise from our definition of "God" (or a lack of "God"), "Who is God?" seems like a good question to begin with. It also has to be the most difficult and dangerous question in the history of mankind. Searching for the answer to that age-old question has led to countless murders and seemingly endless violence throughout history, both in Christendom and outside of the faith.[3]

In this section, I want to discuss the same violent gods Hardin takes issues with, in the above quote. The first question I ponder: *Where does this view of violence come from?* It is my firm belief that when one approaches Scripture as if it is the dictated word of God; when one believes everything attributed to God in Scripture is 100 percent accurate, then they will be lead to believe in a dualistic god. God is *this* and God is *that* and ends up appearing Janus-faced[4] and schizophrenic. For example: *God loves but he is also wrathful: merciful, but just.* This seems to portray the Father as bi-polar; hell-bent on having his revenge, his retribution, and fulfilling his vengeful wrath on some, while showering others with the riches of everlasting bliss. With this hermeneutic,[5] God becomes implicated in all sorts of madness. Hence, *some* fundamentalists even make bigoted signs and stand on street corners . . . proclaiming God's hatred of his enemies.[6] Others, like the late Jerry Falwell, in a piece with Jesse Jackson on CNN, attempts to justify retributive violence in God's name by saying: "You've got to kill the terrorists before the killing stops. And I'm for the President to chase them all over the world. If it takes ten years, blow them all away in the name of

---

2. Hardin, "Must God Be Violent?," para. 30.

3. Whether Christianity, Judaism, or Islam; God is all too often presupposed as violent and retributive toward the enemies of each faith. I would like to acknowledge, however, this is due to what I would consider poor hermeneutics, rather than the overall thrust of each faith's Scripture. As I will explain throughout part two of this book, if God is believed to be violent, his followers will more than likely follow suit.

4. Janus is the Roman god of "beginnings and transitions": portrayed as having two faces.

5. *Hermeneutics*: the branch of knowledge that deals with interpretation, especially of the Bible or literary texts.

6. This is a reference to the Westboro Baptist Church.

the Lord."[7] While Jerry Falwell and the Westboro Baptist Church are extreme examples, you can witness the effects of the belief in a violent God in local churches everywhere.[8] This is the product of dogmatic exclusivism, Christian or otherwise.

When I began searching for the answer to the question, "Who is God?," I became more and more frustrated that reconciling my understanding of the Father throughout Hebrew Scripture with the personhood of Jesus in the New Testament was impossible. Frankly, some of the Father's attributes and behaviors seemed downright terrifying, or as the Westminster Confessions of Faith states, his judgments are "just and terrible."[9] Ezekiel 25:27 reads: "I will carry out great vengeance on them and punish them in my wrath. Then they will know that I am the Lord, when I take vengeance on them." (NIV) If Jesus revealed the true nature of God during his short life on Earth, how was I to explain the violence attributed to his Father in the Old Testament? I struggled in vain for years as I was never able to understand how God, who is love (1 John 4:8), could obliterate or command Israel to destroy countless people throughout history. Take, for instance, the story of Israel's destruction of the Canaanites; found in the books of Deuteronomy, Joshua, and Judges.

After the Israelites' forty-year punishment in the desert, they are ordered to finally establish residence in the chosen land promised to Abraham.[10] If they encounter a city *on their way* to Canaan, their instructions are as follows and found in chapter twenty of Deuteronomy:

- Offer terms of peace (20:10).

- If peace is accepted, enslave all of the people (20:11).

- If peace is rejected, kill all of the men (20:13) and take the women, children, and livestock as "booty" (20:14).

---

7. This quote is from a debate in 2006 on CNN between Jesse Jackson and Jerry Falwell. The transcript in its entirety can be located at http://www.cnnstudentnews.cnn.com/TRANSCRIPTS/0410/24/le.01.html.

8. For one example: in a piece for *The Raven Foundation*, I discuss how a local church I formerly attended ran a Bible study, using Chris Kyle of "American Sniper" fame as an analogy for how we are to be "sheepdogs." In their praise of this gentleman, one attendee uttered the phrase "they [the Muslim terrorists] are rabid dogs and rabid dogs need to be put down." The essay, in its entirety, can be found at https://www.ravenfoundation.org/the-idolatry-of-violence/.

9. From "Of God and of the Holy Trinity" in the *Westminster Confession of Faith*.

10. See Genesis 15:18.

However, once the Israelites *reach* their chosen land, their instructions are slightly different and even more brutal. They are as follows:

- Offer no terms of peace (20:16).

- Kill all of the men, women, children, and livestock (20:17).

- Do so to resist being tempted by their "detestable" behavior (20:18).

While the Israelites do not completely carry out God's instructions (found in the books of Joshua and Judges), what they were "ordered" to do should make one's stomach turn. Put them anywhere but the Bible and my guess is most Evangelicals would condemn such genocidal commands. However, because these "mandates" *are* located in the Bible, and believed to be from God himself, they often argue the case is settled. However, if you are like me, this simply does not sit well—issues still linger. I believe we must be willing to approach Scripture with our critical thinking caps on: willing to delve deeper to understand what exactly was taking place when these books were written.

The questions remain: How does one resolve these texts that state, over and over, that God kills and directs others to kill, countless human beings? How does one resolve the fact that a literal reading of Scripture renders God's nature highly retributive? What "lens" then do we view the entirety of Scripture through and what story is the Bible telling? How can Christianity, as a whole, begin to take the Gospel account as seriously as it takes the entirety of Scripture? I believe these questions deserve honest answers—answers that are the product of deep reflection.

Now, before anyone accuses me of Marcionism—wanting to simply abandon the Old Testament in its entirety—please hear me out, for I am not a Marcionite. However, I do empathize with the urge to abandon the Hebrew Scriptures if a flat reading is all one is familiar with. In chapter 4, I will begin to offer a way of interpreting human behavior, and thus, interpreting the many strange and epic events of the Old Testament. *I will not be tossing it out though!* This approach is vital because if we ask "Who is God?" before "Who is man?" how can we not end up creating a god of our own design? We must discover who we are before we make any attempt to put our finger on God. For many, this will require a change in one's mind (*metánoia*)—a willingness to step outside of the box of institutionalized religion. However, once this occurs, I believe there will be no going back. In the following section, I would like to focus on a few other presuppositions that remain commonplace throughout Western Christianity.

JUSTICE . . . RETRIBUTIVE OR RESTORATIVE?

If we focus our attention on the doctrine of "hell," I believe the entire discussion could potentially hinge on one major concept; namely, the understanding of God's "justice." The most common response to universal salvation has to do with the seeming lack of justice in the doctrine. Many would share in Wayne Jackson's concerns when he writes: "If the doctrine of universal salvation were true, it would make no difference what anyone believed, taught, or practiced—however bizarre, untrue, or destructive. The consequence of all religious and moral activity would be identical ultimately."[11] Before I address Jackson's unease, I must admit his statement has some truth in it. Indeed, it does not matter what I believe, teach, or practice *in the sense* that God will never stop loving me, never stop pursuing me, and never give up on me. I may conjure up bizarre, untrue, and destructive ideas and yet; God's loving-kindness is said to be everlasting (Psalm 136:1). That being said; Jackson's stance seems contingent on defining the Father's justice as "retributive," as opposed to "restorative."[12] Presupposing a retributive god, one could conclude universal reconciliation lacks a certain "justice," but like I said only a few pages ago, we have to properly *define our terms.*

The Father's justice, I will argue, is for the purpose of correction (*kólasis,* in Greek), grounded in his love for his children. Humanity's justice, the "eye for an eye" variety, is most often retributive. Throughout history, including that of the Jewish people as recorded in what we now call the Old Testament; man often finds a way of viewing the Father as one who takes vengeance on enemies, returning violence with violence. In part two, I will discuss the trajectory of Scripture, one that ebbs and flows into an understanding of what divine justice actually looks like. I will attempt to reconcile key attributes of God and argue everything should be viewed in the context that he does not merely love; he is the very essence of love (1 John 4:8). Thus, the notion that love is somehow in competition with justice seems less than compelling, as no loving father withholds justice when disciplining his children. "All discipline for the moment seems not to be joyful, but sorrowful; yet to those who have been trained by it, afterwards it yields the peaceful fruit of righteousness" (Hebrews 12:11). It is because of

11. Jackson, "The Growing Trend toward Universalism," para. 32.

12. I will argue, because retribution hinges on the notion that "the punishment fits the crime," the retribution model does not work as an argument for eternal conscious torment. A finite number of sins should not require infinite punishment. For punishment to be purely retributive, the punishment must fit the crime.

a parent's love that justice must be a part of a loving relationship. Throughout the entirety of this book, whether discussing what it means to be human, or how God will deal with the wicked, justice will be an important theme. I believe we do ourselves an injustice when we simply presuppose our human way of doing something is synonymous with God's way. Isaiah 55:8–9 states: "For my thoughts are not your thoughts, nor are your ways my ways, says the Lord. For as the heavens are higher than the earth, so are my ways higher than your ways and my thoughts than your thoughts." (NRSV) Justice seems to be one of those concepts Western Christianity has presupposed as "retributive"—purely punitive. I hope to show this assumption to be false.

APATHETIC GOD, APATHETIC BELIEVERS

A common complaint I have heard about the doctrine of universal reconciliation is "it will lead to apathy." If God's justice is presupposed as *retributive,* then the doctrine of universal reconciliation may seem to suggest God is apathetic about sin; a "god made in our own image" as is often accused. If God is apathetic toward sin, people will be "off the hook (eternally)" and free to live their lives of sinful bliss. In other words, *Universalism allows some to have their cake and eat it too.* First, and I realize this is anecdotal, but I do not know a single follower of Christ who really believes this to be true. Second, as I will discuss in chapter 8, punishment does serve a purpose in Universalist theology.

On a personal note, I believe the accusation that "Universalism leads to apathy" is degrading. Not only am I, as a Universalist, not intellectually apathetic (I am trying to read as much as I can), but I find myself quicker to forgive and apologize; yet slower to anger and hostility. I now reason: *If God can find a way to reconcile with all who have sinned against him, so too can I do that in my own life.* In chapter 4, when I introduce mimetic theory, I will also explain why my belief in the God of incomprehensible forgiveness has aided my ability to *preemptively forgive* others as Jesus did.

On the flip side, mimetic theory also brilliantly explains the horribly unfortunate political and social mess humanity is in today. Our mimicry of the vast array of retributive gods is the foundational cause of most of our continual wars, human rights violations, and secondary ecological disasters. We witness this all too often within the most fundamentalist sects of all religions, primarily in Christianity and Islam, but certainly not only within these two faiths.

BEFORE MOVING FORWARD, LET US LOOK BACK

There are plenty more presuppositions most Christians, including myself at one point, believe without ever learning why or where those assumptions came from.[13] One of these presuppositions is "eternal conscious torment[14] as *hell*." When books such as Rob Bell's *Love Wins* are published, pastors are all too quick to reject them as heretical, so as to not allow them to gather any momentum in their mainstream churches.[15] To the questioning mind, it is impossible not to wonder, *"Why?"* The truth will stand up to all scrutiny, no matter how hard-pressing.

In the following chapter, I will touch on some of the more important events and leaders throughout church history. In doing so, I hope to show two things: first, Universalism was an accepted doctrine throughout the first 500 years of Christendom, and second, the doctrine of eternal conscious torment was foundational for the terrifying church/state politics witnessed throughout the church's history. The word "heretic" would become justification for the murders of far too many people. Incorrect theology was a matter of life and death; and church was too often judge, jury, and executioner.

---

13. I have personally heard a three-year old girl say "If you don't believe in Jesus, you go to jail." Now, would any rational person conclude she is able to reason through matters related to soteriology or eschatology? I think not.

14. For purposes of this book, I will define "eternal conscious torment," or simply, "eternal torment," as a place of everlasting physical and/or spiritual suffering, separated from the presence of God.

15. The same thing could be said about Edward Fudge's *The Fire that Consumes*, first published in 1982. In it, Fudge challenges the Western doctrine of hell, arguing in favor of annihilationism instead.

2

A Brief Look into the
History of Christianity

SOME MAY BELIEVE THAT universal reconciliation is a modern movement, rooted more in secular humanism than in the teachings of Jesus of
Nazareth, the Apostles, and the early church fathers. This could not be further from the truth, for even St. Augustine, whom I will discuss later in this
chapter, acknowledged that "indeed very many" did not believe in eternal
damnation.[1] In modern times, Universalists are often accused of abandon-
ing the Bible because of outside, "worldly" pressures. For many Christians,
my theology is unfairly seen as a way to fit in with the "liberal" culture of
the time, rather than the traditions of the church. In this chapter, I will discuss where Universalism fits in with the history of Christianity as a whole.

THE APOSTLES' CREED

If you read the Apostles' Creed, which dates back as far as 250—350 CE
and is the earliest known declaration of the Christian faith; you will find
it makes no mention of any punishment that is eternal, conscious, or tor-
menting. In fact, it makes no mention of punishment what so ever. The
following is the Apostles' Creed, in its entirety. (Note: the "common" print
is the Greek portion, written as early as 250 CE, while the "italic" print was

---

1. Augustine, *Enchiridion*, sec. 112.

added as late as 359 CE by the Western Church, and was in Latin).[2] I will explain why the Latin language is significant later in this chapter.

> I believe in God the Father Almighty (*maker of heaven and earth*) and in Jesus Christ his only son our Lord, who was (*conceived*) by the Holy Ghost, born of the Virgin Mary, suffered under Pontius Pilate, was crucified (*dead*) and buried, (*he descended into hell*). The third day he arose again from the dead; he ascended into heaven and sitteth at the right hand of (*God*) the Father (*Almighty*). From thence he shall come to judge the quick and the dead. I believe in the Holy Ghost, the Holy (*Catholic*) Church, (*the communion of the saints*) the forgiveness of sins; the resurrection of the body, (*and the life everlasting*). Amen.[3]

As creedal statements progress throughout history, their complexities grow, and more specific theologies take hold. The earliest Greek creed incrementally evolves into the Athanasian Creed in 500 CE, which includes the phrase, "they that have done evil, into everlasting fire."[4] In a few hundred years, more and more doctrinal statements had to be affirmed in order to be western orthodox, including what appears to be "everlasting punishment."

THE FIRST UNIVERSALISTS

For the first 300 years of Christianity, a common view was that *God would reconcile all mankind in the end*. Between 170 and 430 CE, of the six theological schools in existence, four taught universalism, one taught annihilationism and one (Rome) taught eternal conscious torment.[5] Arguably the premier theological school of this era (*Patristic*, c. 100—450 CE) was the Catechetical School of Alexandria, based in Alexandria, Egypt.[6] Many of the members of the school, including Clement of Alexandria (150–215 CE) and his successor Origen (185–254 CE) affirmed universal salvation. Both were great thinkers and theologians and were as influential as any during the first few centuries.

2. Hanson, *Universalism,* Ch. 1, para. 2.

3. Ibid.. para. 5.

4. You can find the *Athanasian Creed* at https://www.ccel.org/creeds/athanasian.creed.html.

5. Hanson, *Universalism,* Ch. 11, para. 17.

6. Stetson, "The History of Universalism," para. 11.

Origen, for instance, was one of the great philosophical minds of the third century. J.W. Hanson writes of Origen:

> This greatest of all Christian apologists and exegetes, and the first man in Christendom since Paul, was a distinct Universalist. He could not have misunderstood or misrepresented the teachings of his Master. The language of the New Testament was his mother tongue. He derived the teachings of Christ from Christ himself in a direct line through his teacher Clement; and he placed the defense of Christianity on Universalist grounds.[7]

Although some of Origen's beliefs were condemned, such as the pre-existence of souls, his universalism was not one of them . . . until much later.

Origen's predecessor, Clement of Alexandria, seems to affirm the same Universalist theology when he writes:

> And how is he Savior and Lord and not Savior and Lord of all? But he (Christ) is the Savior of those who have believed, because of their wishing to know, and of those who have not believed he is Lord, until by being brought to confess him they shall receive the proper and well-adapted blessing for themselves which comes by him.[8]

Even Gregory of Nyssa (330–395 CE), who was a prominent proponent of the Nicene Creed and the concept of the Trinity, was a devout Universalist. He is to Eastern Orthodoxy what Augustine is to the West. In a book entitled *Sermo Catecheticus Magnus*, Gregory of Nyssa writes:

> The annihilation of evil, the restitution of all things, and the final restoration of evil men and evil spirits to the blessedness of union with God, so that He may be 'all in all,' embracing all things endowed with sense and reason.[9]

This certainly is not an exhaustive survey of early church beliefs. The point is, as Augustine acknowledged, there were "indeed many" who affirmed universal salvation. I have mentioned a few of the more prominent names in order to show the doctrine of universal reconciliation has been around, and in fact was somewhat prominent, since the beginning of the church.

---

7. Hanson, *Universalism*, Ch. 10, para. 6.
8. Ibid., Ch. 9, para. 30.
9. Stetson, "The History of Universalism," para. 22.

CHRISTIANITY AND THE STATE

Christendom does not witness a major push toward a monopoly on thought until Rome makes Christianity legal in 313 CE. Constantine, a Roman emperor, purportedly had a vision prior to the Battle of the Milvian Bridge, which was instrumental in his rise as sole Emperor of Rome. This vision, which was reported to have been a "cross of light" with the Greek words, "*Ἐν Τούτῳ Νίκα, En toutō níka*" (translating to, "In this sign, you shall conquer"), allegedly gave Constantine the courage to win the battle for the Christian God.[10] Constantine indeed converted to Christianity and during his political reign, Roman politics merged with the Christian faith. Where there is Roman politics, there is empire and war . . . chariots and swords . . . war and death. Christian history after Constantine would be no different. I will not go into the gory details of the history of violence from within the church, but as most would admit, it does not exactly resemble something like the Sermon on the Mount.

When Christianity merged with Rome, the language of the Western church also shifted. Latin became the dominant language of many of the church leaders—although Greek remained dominant in the East. Without this Latin influence, Augustine of Hippo (354–430 CE), who is considered by many to be the greatest theologian in history, would possibly never have amounted to much within theological circles as he did not study much Greek.

Augustine held to the belief that non-Christians were destined to an eternity of fiery torture. This dualistic ending to the human drama is quite similar to that of Manichean Gnosticism, in which Augustine has his background in.[11] Because of this belief, he seemed to embrace inflicting violence against those deemed "heretic," since, in his mind, heretics murdered the souls of those around them.[12] Augustine argues:

10. If this vision is indeed accurate, it is my opinion Constantine misinterpreted the words shown to him, as any conquering that occurred through the cross was a peaceful conquering of sin, not a conquest through military might. However, and not of importance with regards to this book, I find the alleged vision (in the way it was reported) to be false.

11. In Manichaeism, there is the belief in a dualistic nature of the universe. The spiritual world is good, while the material world is evil. In the world of darkness, there resides an eternal evil being and his cohorts, which include references to the fallen angels from the Book of Enoch.

12. Talbott, *Inescapable Love of God*, 24.

> But we have shown that Paul was compelled by Christ; therefore the Church, in trying to compel the Donatists, is following the example of her Lord . . . Wherefore, if the power [of the sword] which the Church has received by divine appointment in its due season, through the religious character and faith of Kings, be the instrument by which those who are found in the highways and hedges—that is, in heresies and schism—are compelled to come in, then let them not find fault because they are compelled.[13]

In other words, to coerce the Donatists through physical force was simply "following the example of [the] Lord."[14] To Augustine (who was admittedly brilliant and in one sense, simply a product of his time) and others, the sin of heresy was weighted far worse than the sin of murder. So, to save the multitudes from the deceptions of the heretics, death had to be applied liberally in order for some souls to be saved from their eternal deception. Without the doctrine of eternal damnation, this line of thinking could not have had the power over the multitudes that it did. Indeed, the fear and terror employed by the Roman Empire and eventually the Roman Catholic Church were instrumental in suppressing the masses that were under their reign.

While it is Augustine's theology of hell that remains the greatest influence in the West (cemented primarily by *City of God* and *Handbook*),[15] it was Justinian's sixth-century anathemas (of universal reconciliation) that cemented the doctrine of eternal torment as orthodox from henceforth.[16] From this point on, it would be much more difficult to take a pilgrimage in theology, as Karl Barth would put it, with such anathemas. Fear becomes a great controlling force and while church history is filled with great and inspirational men and women, she also has a history of intimidation and persecution. This would be only the beginning, as she continues to persecute

13. Augustine, *De Correctione Donatistarum 22*, 633–51.

14. Talbott, *Inescapable Love of God,* 24.

15. Machuga, *Three Theological Mistakes,* 224. *City of God*, for instance, is not written until the fifth century, roughly 400 years after the life of Christ. To put this in perspective, Augustine is as removed from Christ as we are from French King Louis XIV, Sir Isaac Newton, Galileo Galilei, and John Calvin.

16. In fact, the council where Universalism was officially condemned was called—not by the Bishop of Rome—but by the Roman Emperor Justinian in 553 CE. Because of controversy over some of Origen's beliefs, namely the preexistence of souls, the doctrine of 'apokatastasis' was anathematized not only by Justinian in 543 CE, but also at the Fifth Ecumenical Council of Constantinople in 553 CE. See Morwenna Ludlow's essay "Universalism in the History of Christianity" in *Universal Salvation?*, 193.

to this day. I even wonder, had *this book* been published during someone like Augustine's life, what my fate would have been. Or, perhaps he could have lived during the twentieth century and possessed tanks, bombs, gas chambers, and Blitzkrieg to silence those who he disagreed with on matters of complex theology. It sometimes seems one group's idea of a "saint" is another group's idea of a "Hitler."[17]

During the thousand year middle ages, the Roman Catholic Church did their best to keep Scripture in Latin—a language not understood by commoners. The standard form of the Bible was the *Latin Vulgate*, translated by Latin priest St. Jerome (347–420 CE). Ironically, at one point St. Jerome was a Universalist who even believed "the Apostate Angel" (Lucifer) would return to his "first estate."[18] He would later recant this idea, however. Essentially, it was this translation that was the only version of Scripture available in Western Europe, and it was not comprehensible for anyone but Latin clergy and scholars. When the *Latin Vulgate* was completed circa 405 CE, *Hádēs, Sheol, Gehenna, and Tartaróō* were all translated into "*infernum*," which in turn would later be translated into "hell."

Think about that—words that did not mean "eternal conscious torment" to *all* Second Temple Jews[19] (the people whom Jesus lived among—more on them later) now simply read "hell" in Scripture that the common man did not have access to in its original language for roughly one thousand years. So, when someone now reads "hell" in Scripture, the "hell" that comes to mind in the West is a medieval, Dante's *Inferno* type of idea, not necessarily a Second Temple Jewish one.

THE REFORMATION

Martin Luther (1483–1546 CE), who is considered by many to be the "father of the Reformation," was the key figure in the movement away from

---

17. This is not to suggest that Augustine should be deemed as '"bad" as a Hitler. However, what I am attempting to suggest is that given different circumstances, any one of us, including those we deem saintly, could be what society deems a monster. Augustine was correct on some matters of theology, but to justify terror in God's name is a gross misunderstanding of the mission of Christ.

18. Quoted by Giovanni Papini in *The Devil*, 155; see also Talbot, *Inescapable Love of God*, 15.

19. *Second Temple Judaism* is a period in Jewish history marked by the building of the second Holy Temple in 515 BCE and the destruction of Jerusalem by the Romans in 70 CE. This is the period in which Jesus lived and is the context of the New Testament.

the Roman Catholic Church in the West. He rightfully challenged such teachings as: papal and priestly authority in the cancelling of sins, the purchasing of salvation, and much more. Although his *Ninety-Five Theses* was not meant to be the publication it turned out to be, for Luther, it *was* high time someone questioned the more grotesque practices of the church.

For the purposes of this book, however, I want to briefly focus on Luther's introduction to the idea of a *theologia crucis*, or "theology of the cross"—contained in his *Heidelberg Theses*, numbers 19–21.[20] Luther writes: "He deserves to be called a theologian, however, who comprehends the visible and manifest things of God seen through suffering and the cross."[21] In essence, what we know about God begins at the cross, revealed in Jesus. Many great theologians have expanded on this idea of a "theology of the cross," but could not have done so without Luther's insights. In chapter 5, I will offer my view of the Atonement, fully agreeing with Luther that what we know about God must begin with the mercy witnessed at the cross.

Although Luther had his darker side, such as his anti-Semitism, he brought many new and revolutionary ideas to the church. We must remember, all people are products of their time. We must be willing to embrace the positive ideas such great thinkers develop, while also willing to point out where they may have gone wrong. My friend Michael Hardin once said "we all must be forgiven for our theology." Whether Augustine, Luther, or Calvin: Hardin and Talbott—all have missed the mark in some aspect. I certainly do not claim to have a "perfect theology." Nobody should.

Because I mentioned John Calvin in the last paragraph, I would now like to broadly mention his major contributions to Christian thought, as well as what seemed like his "dark side." In the following chapter, I will then discuss his theology more specifically. First, Calvin was one of the most brilliant Christian thinkers in history and is most responsible for thinking about theology as a system—one that attempts to think about God in orderly and rational ways. Second, he wanted to make sure people thought about God's grace in a different manner than the direction many were going; where synergism[22] was a part of salvation. Thus, he believed God saves everyone He wants and that some were elected to be with him forever and

---

20. Luther, "Heidelberg Disputation."

21. Ibid., thesis # 20.

22. In theology, *synergism* is the doctrine that states salvation is contingent on cooperation between God's grace and human freedom.

some were not. Calvin's exclusivist theology, then, seemed to play a large role in his behavior and ethics.

Like Luther and Augustine, Calvin's "dark side" involved violence and persecution. Under Calvin, referred to as the "Pope of Geneva" by his contemporary Sebastian Castellio,[23] many who were found guilty of blasphemy were put to death. Although it was the state and not the church that was the authority on who lived and who died, the two did not seem at odds with each other under Calvin's leadership. In fact, I will point to one such instance where we witness this.

Many are familiar with the infamous clash between Calvin and Michael Servetus (1511–1553 CE). Calvin believed Servetus to be a heretic due to his non-Trinitarian beliefs, and in-line with the Roman Catholic Church during the middle ages; he believed that *heretics deserved to die*. It is true that Calvin did not want Servetus killed in such a gruesome manner (by being burned at the stake with green wood, so as to burn at a slower and more torturous pace); he does make it clear, however, in the following portion of a letter, that he wanted Servetus dead:

> Servetus lately wrote to me and coupled with his letter a long volume of his delirious fancies, with the Thrasonic boast that I should see something astonishing and unheard of. He would like to come here if it is agreeable to me. But I do not wish to pledge my word for his safely. For, if he comes, I will never let him depart alive, if I have any authority.[24]

As I will go into great detail in part two, people will imitate others, especially the behaviors they believe God engages in. In light of this, it should start to become clear why Calvin and Augustine justified acts of terror in God's name.[25] Where Augustine had the Donatists, Calvin had Servetus. The characters were different, but the theology and the acts of violence were quite similar.

---

23. Ebenezer, *Understanding the Gift of Salvation*, 246.

24. Talbott, *Inescapable Love of God*, 23—original quote from Parker, *John Calvin*, 118.

25. Acts of terror in "God's name" are still justified today. Some, like what groups such as ISIS advocate, are done brutally and in plain sight. Others, however, hide behind the guise of the democratic process and/or nationalism. The violence is more subtle, but present nonetheless.

CONCLUDING REMARKS

Let me remind you what Wayne Jackson, sharing the view many Christians seem to have on the subject, has to say about Christian Universalism: "If the doctrine of universal salvation were true, it would make no difference what anyone believed, taught, or practiced—however bizarre, untrue, or destructive. The consequence of all religious and moral activity would be identical ultimately."[26] I cannot help but think how bizarre, untrue, and destructive many of the teachings of the church were throughout the early church, middle ages, the Reformation, and still today. And yet, it is my belief that God loves and ultimately forgives the very people who continue to use destructive doctrine to inflict terror in God's name.

This chapter is not meant to discredit the entirety of the works of certain historical church leaders. It also is not an exhaustive account of the history of the church in any way. Also, I fully realize this chapter is not an argument for or against anything theological. My goal, then, is to point out that the histories of some of the men the church nearly worships as demigods are not as pristine as they would like to admit.[27] We should view the great thinkers of the past in the context of their culture and the time period in which they lived. Many theologians offered great insights throughout their lives, but also cemented what I would consider incorrect doctrines. I hope to point that out, beginning in the following chapter.

26. Jackson, "The Growing Trend toward Universalism," para. 32.

27. For more on this, including the Reformers' persecution of the Anabaptists, see Hardin, *Jesus Driven Life*, 123–25 and Talbott, *Inescapable Love of God*, 24–26.

3

One God, Three Competing Views

I WOULD LIKE TO conclude part one by discussing the competing systems of belief vis-à-vis the doctrine of salvation. I will not focus an inordinate amount of energy discussing the minute details of each system of theology, as the goal will not be to draw any strong conclusions per se. However, my focus instead will be to model how assuming one system of theology over another, prior to hearing the arguments, is *fallacious*. Both Arminians (named after Jacob Arminius 1560–1609 CE) and Calvinists have, generally, focused their attention on only these two doctrines, leaving "Universalism" in the "untouchable" category. As I mentioned in the previous chapter, because of the likes of Augustine and Justinian, the doctrine of universal reconciliation has been all but buried under nearly two millennia of church history and politics. However, that seems no reason to assume the Universalist stance as incorrect, for we *essentially* believe core doctrines from both Arminianism and Calvinism, yet are deemed "heretics" by the majority of the church. This makes no sense to me. I will point this out throughout this chapter, drawing primarily from philosopher Thomas Talbott, whose work was my first introduction into this type of thinking, so I must give credit where credit is most certainly due.

ARMINIANISM VS. CALVINISM

Before I compare and contrast all three major systems of soteriology within Christianity, I wanted to introduce the two mainstream views; namely,

Arminianism and Calvinism (or Augustinianism). In the following table, I will broadly cover the "Five Points" within each system (with anything, there will be various differences amongst various Arminians and Calvinists—*these will be broad definitions*). After doing so, I will discuss what I see as the weaknesses of each before introducing "Talbott's Triad," which aptly exposes what I believe to be faulty reasoning.

Five Points of Arminianism	Five Points of Calvinism
Free Will After the fall, human nature was greatly affected. However, man still has the freedom to affirm or deny Christ as his Savior. We can do "good" or "evil," but are not enslaved to sin. If we are "saved," we take part in our salvation by having faith in Jesus Christ.	*(T)otal Depravity* After the fall, man became unable to believe the gospel. As sinners, we are 100 percent corrupt—rotten to the core. We are evil, maniacal, and deceitful. In every case, man will choose evil over good. We contribute nothing toward salvation—it is a free gift from God.
Conditional Election As believers, our election is determined by God's foreknowledge that we would freely believe the gospel. Everyone is offered the choice to believe or not but affirming Jesus Christ is the cause of salvation.	*(U)nconditional Election* God selected certain people before the foundation of the world to be saved. His choosing is solely based on his sovereign will and any faith that happens after is not of man's choosing whatsoever. In the end, God chooses whom to save and whom not to save.
Universal Redemption (not *that* kind) It is *possible* for everyone to be saved based on what Christ did on the cross. However, salvation is actualized by belief. We have to choose to accept reconciliation.	*(L)imited Atonement* Christ died for everyone the Father meant to save. Christ's death was a substitution for the just deserts some sinners had coming to them.
Resistible Grace Because man is free, so too is he free to reject even the Holy Spirit. First, we must believe. Then, the Spirit can make us new.	*(I)rresistible Grace* The Holy Spirit extends herself to the elect and cannot be thwarted. The Spirit causes the sinner to repent 100 percent of the time.
Falling from Grace The "saved" can lose salvation if they do not persevere in their faith.	*(P)erseverance of the Saints* Those who are "saved" are kept that way by the Father and so they persevere until death.

As I will discuss in the following section, each soteriological system has biblical support. I will not go into extraordinary detail for each as that is not the primary point of this chapter or book. However, it is important to understand what Arminians and Calvinists each believe because Universalists *essentially* believe portions of each.

WESTERN THEOLOGY'S SHAKY LOGIC

Calvinists inevitably charge the Arminians with downplaying the sovereignty of God while Arminians point out that Calvinists lessen his unconditional love. Thankfully, there is a third option, one that acknowledges both God's unending love for all of humanity and his ultimate sovereignty. Philosopher Thomas Talbott, in his book *The Inescapable Love of God*, lays out three inconsistent sets of propositions, all appearing to have *prima facie* biblical support. He argues that all three cannot logically co-exist and that one must be incorrect in spite of said support. I will paraphrase "Talbott's Triad" in the following:

1. *It is God's will to reconcile all sinners to himself.*

2. *God's sovereignty is such that no one can resist him forever, therefore, he will redeem all whom he desires to.*

3. *Some will be eternally separated (either in eternal conscious torment or annihilated altogether) from God.*[1]

Calvinists reject proposition (1) and argue deductively that God accomplishes his will (2), but not all are drawn to him, and thus some are lost forever (3).[2] Arminians reject proposition (2) as they insist that God extends love to everyone (1), but allows some to reject him forever, and these are thus lost as well (3).[3] Universalists deductively reason that God's love indeed extends to all (1) and that he will successfully accomplish redemption for everyone (2) and thus reject proposition (3).[4]

To presume the Universalist stance is incorrect while assuming either the Arminian or Calvinist correct would be "begging the question."[5] One would have to argue proposition (3) has the most biblical evidence but that does not seem to be the case. There in fact seems to be far more evidence for proposition (1) with verses such as 2 Peter 3:9, 1 Timothy 2:4, Romans

1. Talbott, *Inescapable Love of God*, 38.

2. Ibid., 41–42.

3. Ibid.

4. Ibid.

5. *Begging the question*: assuming the conclusion of an argument. This occurs by including the conclusion in one of the premises, often indirectly.

11:32, and Ezekiel 33:11;[6] and proposition (2) with support coming from Ephesians 1:11, Job 42:2, Psalm 115:3, 1 Corinthians 15:27–28, Colossians 1:20, and Romans 5:18;[7] than for proposition (3), which involves passages with translation issues. I will discuss the mistranslations in chapter 8, but regardless, support for this proposition comes from Matthew 25:46 and 2 Thessalonians 1:9.[8]

While simply lining up Bible verses, side by side, to argue one way or another is not an appropriate hermeneutic, the point I am trying to make from paraphrasing "Talbott's Triad," is that Universalists are accused of heresy while using the same deductive reasoning both Arminians and Calvinists employ.[9] The Arminian does not accuse the Calvinist of heresy by accepting propositions (2) and (3) and rejecting (1); nor does the Calvinist charge the Arminian with heresy by accepting proposition (1) and (3) and rejecting (2). However, what remains utterly illogical is that the Universalist is deemed a "heretic" by accepting two propositions, (1) and (2), which are in and of themselves not deemed heresy by either Arminians or Calvinists.[10]

---

6. Which read, respectively: "The Lord is not slow about his promise, as some count slowness, but is patient toward you, not wishing for any to perish but for all to come to repentance"; "who desires all men to be saved and to come to the knowledge of the truth"; "for God has shut up all in disobedience so that he may show mercy to all."; and "say to them, 'as I live!' declares the Lord God, 'I take no pleasure in the death of the wicked, but rather that the wicked turn from his way and live . . . .'"

7. Which read, respectively: "also we have obtained an inheritance, having been predestined according to his purpose who works all things after the council of his will"; "I know that You can do all things, and that no purpose of Yours can be thwarted"; "but our God is in the heavens; he does whatever he pleases"; "for he has put all things in subjection under his feet . . . when all things are subjected to him, then the son himself also will be subjected to the one who subjected all things to him, so that God may be all in all"; "and through him to reconcile all things to himself, having made peace through the blood of his cross; through him, I say, whether things on earth or things in heaven"; and "so then as through one transgression there resulted condemnation to all men, even so through one act of righteousness there resulted justification of life to all men."

8. Talbott, *Inescapable Love of God*, 39–40. Scripture reads, respectively: "these will go away into eternal punishment, but the righteous into eternal life"; and "these will pay the penalty of eternal destruction, away from the presence of the Lord and from the glory of his power."

9. Again, see Morwenna Ludlow's essay "Universalism in the History of Christianity" in *Universal Salvation* regarding the "heresy" of Universalism.

10. Talbott, "Toward a Better Understanding of Universalism," 11.

SOME INITIAL THOUGHTS ON ARMINIANISM & CALVINISM

My intention in this section is not to provide specific exegesis to make an argument for Universalism; rather, it is simply to offer my preliminary thoughts on both Arminianism and Calvinism. It is my hope that this section is not seen as an attack on anyone, but simply as a critique of two doctrines as I see them. Far too often, Christians (me included at one point) tend to follow the teachings of their local pastors, clergy or family members; who in turn received their ideas from their local pastors, clergy and family members and the cycle of presuppositional thinking continues intergenerationally. My hope is that more Christians back away from this anti-intellectual mindset and begin to enter into discussions with those who hold contrary views.

Arminianism

If I may be blunt, the Arminian understanding of God seems rather impotent and powerless in overcoming evil. He does not seem, as Anselm put it, to be the greatest thing conceived, if his desire to save all (2 Peter 3:9, 1 Timothy 2:4, Romans 11:32, and Ezekiel 33:11) is thwarted by our "will."[11] If Christ died for everyone, then he died for billions of people who are believed by most to be headed straight to hell . . . the Dante's *Inferno* version. Taking a Pauline perspective, Thomas Talbott concludes: "The harder I tried to work out a consistent Arminian theology and to harmonize it with the New Testament writings, the harder I found it to escape the fact that, according to Paul, our final destiny is already foreordained and not a matter of free choice at all."[12] Like Talbott, I too have a very difficult time reconciling the writings of Paul with the idea that we choose our eternal destiny. St. Paul writes: "Also we have obtained an inheritance, having been *predestined* [emphasis mine] according to his purpose who works all things after the council of his will . . . " (Ephesians 1:11). I will expand on Pauline theology in chapter 7; arguing that "all" are in fact *predestined* to be reconciled. Thus, it is my belief that we are "free" to make choices but, as Paul argued, are not

---

11. Anselm argues in *The Proslogion*, chapter 2, that God is "something than which nothing greater can be thought." This is known as "Anselm's Ontological Argument" for the existence of God.

12. Talbott, "Toward a Better Understanding of Universalism," 4.

free from our own sinful nature (see Romans 6:20). I cannot help but think how this begs the question: *If we are enslaved to something, how can we have free will?* As Christians, if we are going to discuss "free will," we would also need to discuss what/whom we are being freed from; and what we are now free to do. I will argue in chapter 4 to have "free will" is to be *free to desire what the Father desires.*

Moreover, how can anyone suggest that a free moral agent would ever *choose* hell over heaven? Damnation over salvation? Eric Reitan writes: "We never freely choose what we have no motive to choose and every motive not to choose. Hence, it is incoherent to speak of someone freely choosing damnation. Anyone who does choose damnation must therefore lack genuine freedom."[13] If the "doors of hell are locked on the inside,"[14] as C.S. Lewis put it, would that not suggest "their" wickedness would be due to a disease—a mental illness—slavery to some delusion or illusion, one that would not need retributive punishment, but would need healing from "the spring of the water of life"?[15] God's beauty is such that I cannot fathom any truly healed person "freely" rejecting it. For Arminians though, *the free choice to reject Jesus Christ results in the presupposed notion that God retributively punishes the wicked—retribution for their mental illness, so it seems.*

Maybe the following will be an emotional plea—forgive me if it is— but the idea that I, being the irrational and selfish creature that I am, have any say in my ultimate fate is downright terrifying. *Did not Peter's faith wane when it counted most?*[16] *My hope is that God loves me too much to torture me forever or annihilate me altogether for making an error in judgement—for concluding something other than "Jesus." And, honestly, my greater hope is that God loves all too much to torture my friends and family forever if they make an error in judgment and conclude other than "Jesus." This "choice" seems more influenced by fear than love—an eternal ultimatum if you will. Is God "Creator" or "Destroyer"?* Jürgen Moltmann takes issue with this line of thinking and brings to a fitting close my issues with Arminianism in the following:

> Can some people damn themselves, and others redeem themselves by accepting Christ? If this were so, God's decisions would

---

13. Reitan, "Human Freedom and the Impossibility of Eternal Damnation," 128.

14. Lewis, *Problem of Pain*, 127.

15. See Revelation 21:6.

16. See Luke 22:34; 54–62.

be dependent on the will of human beings. God would become the auxiliary who executes the wishes of people who decide their fate for themselves. If I can damn myself, I am my own God and judge. Taken to a logical conclusion this is atheistic. There is a more modern evangelical idea about a conditional immortality, according to which no one finds a life after death without believing and unless God confers eternal life; all the rest simply remain dead. But I do not find this very helpful either, because it excludes God's judgment. Mass murderers might possibly welcome this solution, because they would then not have to answer before God's judgment for what they had done. The annihilationists think that unbelievers do not go to hell eternally but are simply destroyed and fall into an eternal nothingness; but this too does not seem to me compatible with the coming omnipresence of God and his faithfulness to what he has created. For the lost to 'disappear' conforms to the terrible experiences with the murder squads in military dictatorships, but it does not accord with God. The God of the Bible is the Creator, not simultaneously the Destroyer, like the Indian god Shiva.[17]

Calvinism

In *Calvinist* theology, God predestines some to eternal bliss while billions are eternally tortured (majority view) or annihilated altogether (minority view). Where the Arminian version of God seems willing but powerless to accomplish the restitution of all things, Calvin and Augustine's God is all powerful but unwilling. I just cannot fathom a loving Father predetermining which children he saves from his own vengeful wrath and which he does not. Certainly, then, his love for the elect is greater than his love for the non-elect. I cannot seem to square this with the fact that his very nature *is* Love (1 John 4:8).

Calvinists generally retort by discussing God's "holiness." This is perfectly fine, but like I mentioned before, we have to define our terms. Let me leave you with one last thought regarding how I interpret this supposed "holiness" of the Calvinist understanding of God:

> The Greek word for "holy" is *hágios*, translated to "set apart" in English, and is one of the primary descriptions of God in Calvinist thinking. If the holiness of God is emphasized in this theology,

17. Moltmann, *The Coming of God*, 109.

and it should be, then it certainly begs the question as to how this God is "set apart" if he behaves in the exact same manner as human beings do. His exclusivism rather, seems *far greater* than even that of mankind's.[18] Whereas humans discriminate in temporal ways, God's exclusion is everlasting. Moreover, if God demands the blood sacrifice of his son for the sins of either all mankind, or a portion in this tradition, and then discards the rest into a fiery inferno to be tortured forever, then it seems that God responds *to sin* and violence precisely in the same manner as mankind does, namely, with retribution.

If Calvin's understanding of God is that he does not love his enemies—and I have heard Calvinists actually affirm this—but asks us to love our enemies (Matt. 5:44), how is he the one who is holy? How is he like Jesus? Furthermore, because of this Janus-faced understanding, the only one whom God seems set apart from *is* Jesus. So, who are "the elect" to follow: Jesus or his Father?

In addition to an irreconcilable understanding of the Father and the Son, this system of theology has the potential to create an "us vs. them" mentality—one that history has witnessed time and time again (see Augustine and Calvin). In the previous chapter, I mentioned how our view of God will inevitably impact the way we view others around us. Ex-Calvinist, Steve Jones, explains it in the following:

> Calvinism is one more illustration of the futility of systematic theology. God's truths, particularly relating to soteriology, are too lofty to be put into concise formulae. The Five Points of Calvinism oversimplify the profound truths of God. They derive their force from proof-texts rather than the general tenor of Scripture. More than that, the doctrines frequently create a spirit of division, elitism and theological snobbery. The system erects walls between believers. It creates a class of Christians within the church general who are supposedly part of a worthy 'inner circle.'[19]

A FEW FINAL THOUGHTS

I did not include this chapter to be an end-all argument in favor of universal reconciliation. Rather, I see it as a platform on which to build a better, more

18. Talbott, *Inescapable Love of God*, 12.
19. Jones, "Calvinism Critiqued," para. 7.

consistent view of the Father, Scripture, and what it means to "follow Jesus." I included this chapter because it is the type of argumentation I personally needed so I could see where my theology seemed illogical. My hope is it makes those who tightly hold to their own subjective view question where their doctrines come from, what they say about God, and what they say about the fate of humanity.

As for me, I can now approach the Father with a fresh lens, one that is not tainted with theology passed down intergenerationally from *where, I at one point did not know*? God is the one who compels me to humble myself at the very thought of him. I see God as my "Abba," who sent Christ who suffered, not because the Father needed blood to satisfy his wrath, but because he loves us dearly; because he desperately wants all to join in relationship with him. And because he has the power to get what he wants, I cannot hope for anything other than that he will ultimately save all.

In the following chapter, I will introduce René Girard and mimetic theory, beginning by exploring what it means to be human and how we cannot attempt to make sense of our Heavenly Father without making sense of who we are as human beings. Mimetic theory can help explain why our views of God are the way they are and why it is so important to get God as correct as humanly possible. In the whole of part two, I hope to persuasively argue for a non-violent, non-retributive God—which does not mean he is not severe—who loves all.

PART II

THE GIRARDIAN TRAJECTORY

4

Mimetic Theory and Scripture

WHAT IS SELF?

FOR THE LONGEST TIME, I believed I was an autonomous, "self-owned" individual. I reasoned: "If I could prove this, I could have an identity different from everyone else." However, what I was grasping at simply was not there. It turns out, autonomy is a façade and my identity is defined by my relationships with others. In fact, all identities are defined by their relationship to others. Think about it: you are "human" because you are in relationship with those around you (and because of technological advances, those far from you). This begins moments after a child is born, when a baby will imitate a mother's facial expressions.[1] Jean-Michel Oughourlian explains it is our innate imitation, or mimesis, which is the driving force behind our relationality. He writes:

> No one, to my knowledge, has ever thought of naming the force that draws the child into reproducing what an adult says or does, this force of attraction, interest and attention . . . so much of it taken for granted, so much of it a part of the fabric of humanity. A young child has no power to resist that attraction. To feel such attraction is the child's very nature, to the degree that he or she is 'normal.' A child lacking this capacity would be deprived of something basic to his humanity; he would become isolated, autistic.

1. Meltzoff, *Imitative Mind*. 23.

That natural force of cohesion, which alone grants access to the social, to language, to culture, and indeed to humanness itself, is simultaneously mysterious and obvious, hidden in and of itself, but dazzling in its effects.[2]

Because our "self" is defined by our relationship to the "other," we develop an understanding of "likeness" (which makes relationship possible to begin with) and "otherness" (which gives the space needed to interact relationally).[3] In other words, we can develop relationships because we are able to understand we are "like" our fellow human, but they are an "other" apart from ourselves, and therefore the space between the two individuals is for exchanging the energy needed to develop the relationship. Without this, we cannot define "self." René Girard coined the term "interdividual" to explain this phenomenon.

If I can offer some personal examples, I first think of my relationship with my wife and daughter; as they have the greatest influence over how I define my "self." I am a husband and a father: a friend, mentor, confidant, and counselor. If I expand my "self," I am a son and brother. My mother taught me language and I taught my brother his first curse word. My grandmother's death forced me to grieve and ponder death. My stepdad modeled how to throw a baseball and my dear friend Mike has aided me greatly through my journey in writing this book. I could go on *ad infinitum* but the point is, I am my relationships. *Without them, what else am I?*

Mirror Neurons

I have been labeled a "mimetic theorist" only once, which would make me a scientist I suppose (I say that ironically for *I'm no scientist*). Because I am not a scientist, I will keep this section short. However, I cannot fail to mention a discovery in 1996 that would bridge two fields of science; namely, anthropology and neurophysiology.

The discovery of "mirror neurons" by an Italian team of scientists revolutionized the way we think of human behavior. What they noticed is certain cells would "fire," not only when you clap your hands, but when you witness someone else clapping their hands. In essence, our brain could not tell if we were performing an action, or if we perceived that action. This

---

2. Oughourlian, *Puppet of Desire*, 2—sourced from Rabe, *Desire Found Me*, 23.

3. Rabe, *Desire Found Me*, 32.

phenomenon also occurs when we witness another's *desire* for something. Michael Hardin writes it as follows: "monkey see, monkey do is now monkey see, monkey thinks he do."[4] Like I mentioned just a few paragraphs before, this occurs at birth and is precisely how we learn.

Desire

In our imitation of others, we begin to imitate each other's very desires. As I will explain in the following section, this will eventually lead to conflict; primarily if imitated desire becomes "twisted," like in a case of the placement of prohibitions. However, while desire leads to conflict, it also leads to intimacy. Thus, *desire* is not bad, but human. It gives us our freedom. Girard explains it in the following:

> If our desires were not mimetic, they would be forever fixed on predetermined objects; they would be a particular form of instinct. Human beings could no more change their desire than cows their appetite for grass. Without mimetic desire there would be neither freedom nor humanity.[5]

If mimetic desire is what gives us freedom and defines our "humanity," but is also what causes rivalry and mimetic conflict, then it certainly tells us a lot about what it means to be human. I believe it does all of the above, which is why the Ten Commandments, found in the book of Exodus, are so compelling in their addressing of this.

What is interesting about the tenth commandment, in particular, is unlike numbers six through nine,[6] which deal with the prohibition of actions,[7] commandment number ten deals with the *desire* to do something. It reads: "You shall not covet your neighbor's house; you shall not covet your neighbor's wife or his male servant or his female servant or his ox or his donkey or anything that belongs to your neighbor" (Exodus 20:17). Of the Hebrew word translated "to covet," Girard writes: "The Hebrew term translated as 'covet' means just simply 'desire.' This is the word that designates the desire of Eve for the prohibited fruit, the desire leading to the

4. Hardin, *Jesus Driven Life*, 141.

5. Girard, *I See Satan*, 15.

6. Commandments six through nine read: You shall not murder (Exodus 20:13); you shall not commit adultery (20:14); you shall not steal (20:15); you shall not bear false witness against your neighbor (20:16).

7. In the following section, I will discuss how prohibitions arise.

original sin (. . .) The desire prohibited by the tenth commandment must be the desire of all human beings—in other words, simply desire as such."[8] The command to "not engage in mimetic desire" is the first attempt in history (but certainly *not* the last) to address the root cause of human conflict.[9]

In the following section, I will discuss how human conflict escalates due to the imitation of one another's desires, the scapegoating process, as well as how cultures and religions are formed and why a common practice, that of sacrifice, is consistent throughout the vast majority of them.

MIMETIC CONFLICT

In the following, I will lay out a hypothetical situation all parents, babysitters, grandparents, aunts and uncles . . . or anyone who has ever spent time with children will understand.

> Timmy and Susie are in a room full of toys. What will inevitably happen is within what seems like only a matter of moments, the kids will be fighting over one toy. This occurs regardless of what that particular toy is or how many other toys are in the room. Why? Let's say Timmy sees the shiny yellow block: Susie will nonconsciously imitate Timmy's desire for the block (if Susie is cunning enough, she can even get to the shiny yellow block before Timmy can).[10] Now, the two children have become rivals for the shiny block, even if there are other shiny blocks in the room.

In this scenario, the children may bicker for some time before an adult intervenes. *No harm done!* When this type of situation occurs in the big, bad, and scary world, things start becoming more serious. If two men fight over a lover or two gangs fight over "turf," or, worse yet, two corrupt dictators with nuclear bombs are entangled in a mimetic conflict, we start to see the implications of twisted mimetic desire. Violence has a way of escalating over time—like a ticking time bomb, ready to explode.

8. Girard, *I See Satan*, 7–8.

9. Paul also pays special attention to "covetousness" in Romans 7:7–8.

10. You will notice that as children age into adolescence and their teen years, they will be more subtle in what they desire, especially if the object is scarce. In my years working in group homes, this behavior was commonplace. Resources were scarce. Often times, teens would pretend not to care about scarce items, all the while plotting how they would achieve ownership over an item without their peers noticing. Once a peer would notice their desire for something, it was "game on." Mimetic conflict would be inevitable at that point.

Escalation

I can recall one such "time bomb" at a sporting event in Sacramento, California, some years back. During the event, a classic donnybrook broke out in the stands only a few rows in front of me. It began as nothing more than a few shoves, some heated words—a few guys took their shirts off (which I will never understand)—and before I knew it, approximately twenty people were in a full-fledged throw-down.

Fights like this occur because human beings do not actually return violence with violence, but violence with violence . . . plus a little more. *You slap me; I slap you a little harder. In turn, you slap me back a little harder than that because you are upset that I upped the ante in the first place.* We have all witnessed this happen. This is the mob and it is a dangerous and powerful force—one that has the potential to threaten the survival of the entire community or society.[11] To stem the violence, the community must turn to a third party—a scapegoat—to place all the sins of the people upon in hopes that the cycle of violence will cease, and the community will be spared from its self-destruction.

The Scapegoat

When the mob's all-against-all violence escalates enough so as to threaten the community, they will turn to a scapegoat to place the blame on. The *all-against-all* must now become *all-against-one*. However, for this mechanism to work, the all need to be fully unified against the one. If you think back to May 2, 2011, when Osama Bin Laden was killed, you will remember just how unifying that event was in the United States. Regardless of political ideology or affiliation, American citizens took to the streets to celebrate the mechanism that would bring peace to the country, albeit for a very brief time. While Bin Laden certainly displayed evil behavior and was arguably as wicked as humanly possible, he certainly was not guilty for *all of the violence* committed against the people of the United States. Cohesion, in a country as politically divided as any, became possible because of violence. Michael Hardin explains how this happened well in our past:

> Back in human 'pre-history,' mimetic conflict reached a boiling point and it became necessary to find an outlet for all the hostility onto a random innocent victim. This is the 'originary' event

11. Andrade, *René Girard*, sec. 3.

(Girard's term). The random victim becomes the focal point of the community's aggression and creates the first truly united activity of the community, all against one. Seen in this way, the basis for human social cohesion is violence.[12]

In the minds of the members of the community, the scapegoat is both the cause of conflict and the bringer of peace. Once dead, the community is unified by the blood of the scapegoat. *Finally . . . peace!* But this cannot repeat itself too often or there will be too much bloodshed. This brings me to the first of three "pillars of culture": prohibition.

THE PILLARS OF CULTURE

Pillar I: Prohibition

Once the community becomes privy to that which lead to the conflict in the first place, prohibitions are placed on the most highly desired items. Michael Hardin points out the two primary prohibitions, namely "food and women."[13] From there, humans in various cultures at various times have slapped prohibitions on all manners of items and behaviors. From prohibitions on sexual positions to sexual orientations, to prohibitions on certain plants and alcohol, humans have prohibited and attempted to prohibit nearly everything under the sun. (I should note; these prohibitions will cause *desire* to greatly increase for the item prohibited. History proves what happens when mimetic desire becomes "twisted" by prohibition. In the following section, I will discuss what happens when Eve's desire becomes "twisted" by the prohibition of a certain tree.) Thus, prohibitions become the "cure" and the "poison"; juxtaposed much like the Greek word, *pharmakon*.[14] They are meant to bring about peace, but in their implementing, they increase *desire* for the very thing that caused the conflict in the first place.

---

12. Hardin, "The Scapegoat," para. 8. I do not want the word "random" to cause confusion. What is meant by "random" is that regardless of how ethical or unethical the scapegoat is, the violence against him/her will happen regardless of his or her behavior. Thus, the scapegoat is random in that he or she is not the cause of the ills of that particular society.

13. Hardin, *Jesus Driven Life*, 153.

14. *Pharmakon* can be defined as a "cure" to an ailment, or a "poison" that causes an ailment.

Pillar II: Ritual

In honor of the process that leads to the scapegoat's sacrifice which bestows the community temporary peace, members of the society will begin to participate in the dramatizations of the community-saving event.[15] Festivals, celebrations, and re-enactments honoring the event become ritualized and commonplace. *If killing the scapegoat brought peace to the community, certainly it was pleasing to the gods.* This becomes the process by which sacrificial religion is born. Girard writes:

> Religion is nothing other than this immense effort to keep the peace. The sacred is violence, but if religious man worships violence it is only insofar as the worship of violence is supposed to bring peace; religion is entirely concerned with peace, but the means it has of bringing it about are never free of sacrificial violence.[16]

In other words, the goal of religion—of sacred sacrifice—is peace. However, in its implementation, it is, at its core, violence.

Whereas prohibitions are an attempt to limit violent mimetic conflict, rituals reenact the conflict. Thus, the mechanism for sacrifice is born. Only certain sacrifices—based on the "originary event"[17]—are pleasing to the gods. In other words, depending on how the original "all against one" event took place, that is how the ritualized sacrifices would be modeled by that particular culture and/or religious group.

Pillar III: Myth

Dead men tell no tales. Once the scapegoated victim is dead and has no voice, the stories that follow are written by the community. Because they are written by the community, they tell a story that portrays the victim guilty and the community innocent. In fact, they are the reason language exists in the first place. Because the scapegoat was the "cause" of violence and the "bringer of peace," symbols are given that can have more than one meaning.[18] Thus, it is this ability to create symbolism that leads to language[19],

15. Ibid.

16. Girard, *Things Hidden*, 32.

17. Hardin, "The Pillars of Culture," para. 13.

18. Hardin, *Jesus Driven Life*, 154.

19. Girard, *Things Hidden*, 94.

which leads to the creating of stories and myth—all founded on violence (I will demonstrate in the following section how cities are founded on murder). For the purposes of the remainder of this book, this is the definition I will use for "myth."

In the following sections, I will model how the Bible should be read in light of this understanding of the human condition. If you think back to chapter 1, you should recall that I posed a few questions regarding the violence attributed to God throughout Hebrew Scriptures. However, prior to answering those questions, I thought it important to understand humanity first. If we ask "Who is God?" prior to asking "What does it mean to be human?" we will inevitably create a god of our own design without ever understanding why.

Beginning in the next section and continuing throughout the remainder of the book, I will attempt to articulate my understanding of our Heavenly Father. Specifically, in the following section, I will argue the Hebrew writers used their own myth tales to expose myth; those that predate the Hebrew Scriptures. We can only understand a collection of books and letters if we understand the condition of the people who wrote them. There are many biblical authors, written over thousands of years, in various geographical locations and in vastly different cultures. It is my hope I can paint a picture of scripture that gives it some life and vigor. When the Bible is flattened out as if it was entirely written for twenty-first-century American Christians, it loses the cultural context it is built on.

THE BOOK OF GENESIS

First things first—I do not believe the writers of the book of Genesis are trying to convey the message of a "young Earth," literal talking snakes, the phrase "*Adam and Eve, not Adam and Steve*," or any of that. I will say this about the book: *Genesis is one of the most profound books in the Bible.* Before discussing Genesis, however, I want to mention the Babylonian creation myth *Enuma Elish*, due to the very real possibility that it influenced the writers of the book of Genesis. In fact, the oldest copies of the Babylonian myth are possibly thousands of years BC.[20] The process of compiling the Pentateuch (the first five books of the Old Testament) began with David around 1000 BCE and was not completed until roughly 500 BCE (at the

20. Rabé, *Desire Found Me*, 105.

earliest).[21] This would have been after Israel's exile *into* Babylon (between 586–530 BCE). The Hebrew priests likely would have known the dominant culture's creation story, which makes the non-violent creation story in Genesis so compelling. When read in contrast to the stories that were already around, the Hebrew Scriptures begin to tell an intriguing and fresh version of creation.

Enuma Elish

In the following, I will paraphrase the Babylonian creation myth so I can then highlight the important differences in the Genesis account.

> Two primordial gods, Apsu and Tiamet, engage in a sexual union and give birth to multiple generations of gods who begin to torment Tiamet with their incessant noise. Apsu and Tiamet plan to kill their sons but Ea (the water god) foils their plan and kills Apsu. Ea hires a hero named Marduk, who is given divine powers in order to defeat Tiamet. He defeats Tiamet and uses half of her body to create the heavens and half to create the earth. The blood of Tiamet's commander, Kingu, is used to create mankind.[22]

There are a few things I want to point out before discussing the retort from Hebrew Scripture. The Babylonian account presupposes violent gods with mankind being created from the blood spilled within the council of the gods. Because violence played such a large role within civilizations, the Babylonians had no reason to believe violence was not a part of the divine as well. They also viewed their relationship with the gods as that of slavish servitude, which they superimposed onto their culture. *We serve the gods, but lesser men serve us!* Given the cultural context, this is not a far-fetched conclusion to draw (even if incorrect). In the following section, I will describe, at length, the creation account(s) from the Book of Genesis.

Biblical Creation

Whereas the gods of the tale from *Enuma Elish* follow their violent backstory by creating mankind as an afterthought, the first creation story found

---

21. Ibid.
22. Ibid., 106–10.

in the Book of Genesis is peaceful and determined to be "very good."[23] Violence is not a part of creation and man is not simply made for blind service, but made "in our image, according to our likeness" (Genesis 1:26). As I discussed at the beginning of this chapter, to be "like" another is needed in order to be in relationship with the "other." To be made in the "image" and "likeness" of God is to be made as a copy—made to be in relationship with the original. The priestly writer of the first creation story recognizes our existence as meant for relationship with the God of creation. Genesis 1:27–31 reads:

> God created man in his own image, in the image of God he created him; male and female he created them. God blessed them; and God said to them, 'be fruitful and multiply, and fill the earth, and subdue it; and rule over the fish of the sea and over the birds of the sky and over every living thing that moves on the earth.' Then God said, 'behold, I have given you *every* [emphasis mine] plant yielding seed that is on the surface of all the earth, and *every* [emphasis mine] tree which has fruit yielding seed; it shall be food for you; and to every beast of the earth and to every bird of the sky and to everything that moves on the earth which has life, I have given every green plant for food'; and it was so. God saw all that he had made, and behold, it was very good.

Notice *how* we are made in the image of God—male and female, not simply male. And not only are we made in God's image, but we are to care for the earth, both land and sea, being given every animal to care over and *every* tree that bears fruit. In this first account, God gives and gives freely, not withholding anything. The idea of prohibition is absent.

This retelling of creation flies right in the face of the Babylonian account. The God of the Hebrew people puts humanity first, above all other creatures. Imagine hearing this tale for the first time after what was already "known" about how the world came to be. *What an intriguing introduction to a story in light of all the violence attributed to the gods of those living throughout the entire region!?* In the second narrative, however, some very interesting events take place—events that play out, because of our mimetic nature, rather predictably. However, for the Hebrew writers to notice this is also rather compelling.

---

23. Genesis 1:1—2:3 is the first creation story, while Genesis 2:4–24 is the second.

In the second narrative, which was written by an unknown writer known as "the Yahwist,"[24] we discover a prohibition where in the first, there was none. I will compare what God gives/withholds in the following:

Narrative 1 from Genesis 1:29: "Behold, I have given you . . . *every* tree which has fruit yielding seed." [emphasis mine]	Narrative 2 from Genesis 2:16-17: "The Lord God commanded the man, saying, 'from any tree of the garden you may eat freely; but from the tree of the knowledge of good and evil you shall not eat, for in the day that you eat from it you will surely die.'"

The fact that a prohibition is contained in the second creation account is evidence of the very first pillar of human culture. As I discussed in the previous section, prohibitions arise due to an original "all-against-one" scapegoating event. In other words, where there is a prohibition, there is a violent back-story. Moreover, as I mentioned in the previous section, prohibitions will cause desire to increase for the prohibited item. Eve will soon discover how true this really is.

The Fall

In Genesis 3, we are introduced to the serpent, which Andre Rabé describes as the "perfect metaphor for the twisted cycle of perverted mimetic desire".[25] I contend desire becomes so twisted directly *because* of the first prohibition. Inevitably, due to our mimetic hard-wiring, once Eve is deceived by her desire to "be like God" (3:3), she eats of the fruit, gives it to the man who eats and both are expelled from the garden.[26] What is noteworthy is that sin enters the world, not through Eve, who disobeyed the prohibition of the "tree of knowledge of good and evil," but through Adam. Adam, being made in the image of God, was to imitate him but chose to imitate Eve and thus began the cycle of mimetic conflict we are still in today. After Adam and Eve are expelled from the garden, they conceive two sons and shortly thereafter, civilization is founded on a murder.[27]

24. Hardin, *Jesus Driven Life*, 172.

25. Rabé, *Desire Found Me*, 51.

26. Ibid., 174. Notice how the man scapegoats both God and the woman in 3:12, and the woman follows suit by then blaming the serpent in 3:13.

27. Ibid.

Founding Murder

Genesis 4 is the Biblical version of a founding murder myth, where a civilization or culture will tell a story of how their first city was founded. Take, for instance, the founding of Rome. In this story, twin brothers Romulus and Remus fight over which hill to establish a new city on.[28] Romulus slays his brother and names the city *Roma*, after himself. However, like the creation narrative, the biblical founding murder myth will be a retelling, where the victim is innocent, and the surviving party guilty.

In Genesis 4:4–5, without any initial request from God, Cain and Abel offer sacrifices to him anyway.[29] (As I mentioned prior, prohibition is introduced in Gen. 2:16–17. The introduction of sacrifice is yet another clue that we are dealing with myth, as it is a part of the ritualization process. Thus far, we have a prohibition and now a ritual.) The brothers' belief that God demanded offering eventually led to rivalry and murder. Like Romulus, Cain builds a city shortly after murdering his own brother. Genesis 4:17 reads: "Cain had relations with his wife and she conceived, and gave birth to Enoch; and he built a city, and called the name of the city Enoch." Certainly, it seems less-than-compelling that this is to be a city of only *Cain and a few family members. It has myth written all over it.* Only, as I mentioned prior, the guilty party is rightfully acknowledged in the story.

After the murder, Abel's blood does, however, cry out for postmortem vengeance; yet God does not honor his call for retribution. Genesis 4:15 reads: "So the Lord said to him, 'therefore whoever kills Cain, vengeance will be taken on him sevenfold.' And the Lord appointed a sign for Cain, so that no one finding him would slay him." The assumption that Abel wanted "an eye for an eye" is because that would be the common human response, but God wanted violence to stop dead in its tracks. In only six generations, humanity will reap the fruits of *its* version of justice.

Escalation of Violence

As I mentioned in the previous section, retributive violence is not simply "an eye for an eye," but often "an eye for an eye *plus* something extra."

---

28. The brothers agreed to employ "augury," which is the practice of interpreting omens from observing the flight of birds. This practice was common in ancient Rome.

29. Hardin, *Jesus Driven Life*, 174.

Genesis 4:23–24 tells us how vengeance is returned to anyone, including a child, by a man named Lamech. The verses read:

"Adah and Zillah,
Listen to my voice,
You wives of Lamech,
Give heed to my speech,
For I have killed a man for wounding me;
And a boy for striking me;
If Cain is avenged sevenfold,
Then Lamech seventy-sevenfold."

In spite of God's warning of the dangers of vengeance by his "marking" of Cain in verse 15, human beings still find a way to ramp up the retribution. In fact, this violence escalates in such a way that civilization's very existence is threatened by the time of Noah and the flood.

The Flood

The story of Noah and the ark is a very similar tale to the *Epic of Gilgamesh*. The earliest tablets that contain portions of the epic Babylonian poem are dated as far back as 2000 BCE, roughly 1000 years before the Pentateuch (the first five books of the Old Testament) began to be compiled. In the following columns, I will very briefly summarize each tale.

The Epic of Gilgamesh	The Biblical Flood
The god Enlil became so upset over humanity's loudness he convinced the council of gods to destroy all of mankind (how can they sleep with such racket?). One of the gods, Ea, warned Ut-Naphishtim and told him to build an ark and save some of the humans and animals.	The earth was "corrupt" and "filled with violence" and the Lord was sorry that He had created man. God destroys all of mankind, save for Noah and his family and some animals.

I will not go into what the flood, or deluge, scientifically was or was not. For my purposes, the point to understand is the account of the flood found in the Old Testament is another retelling of a Babylonian myth. However, in the Jewish account, God grieves over the corruption of humanity (Genesis 6:6) and after the epic event, offers a promise to never again destroy mankind in such a manner (Genesis 9:15). Again, we see a view of God that shows love and compassion for creation. This was a new concept in the Middle East.

The most important difference I want to point out is the reasons the flood happened in the first place. Whereas the Babylonian myth blames humanity's *infernal hullabaloo* for the flood, the Bible attributes it to "violence" and "corruption" (Genesis 6:11). Michael Hardin illustrates: "To be corrupt and full of violence is one and the same thing; this is what scholars call parallelism in Hebrew writing."[30] The writers are placing emphasis on just how grotesque civilization was at that point.

There are some who insist the biblical flood account is the only one of its kind. This is simply not true. The Bible, however, subverts other myths and hence, because of humanity's *corruption and violence*, the flood can be seen as salvific, as the violence "in the days of Noah" consumed humanity. Without it, the human project could have easily failed. Some may ask, "Well, why did God kill so many people in the first place?" That is a fair question. My short answer is: "He didn't." What I am suggesting in my interpretation of the flood is that the Hebrew writers were attempting to retell an *already existing myth*, one that begins to define an understanding of God that is contrary to their Babylonian counterparts.

The Book of Genesis, when read in light of what we know about mimetic desire, presents a compelling retelling of a story about who we are and who God is. One could say the book is "God-breathed."[31] For the first time in history, people are offered a story of creation that does not involve deceit and murder amongst the gods. Instead, there is an introduction to God that gives freely. There is a new view of God, one that is on the side of all of humanity.

I could have covered the book in more depth, including the story of the family of Abram, concluding with Joseph's forgiveness of his treacherous brothers, but for now, I wanted to keep my analysis of Genesis brief. Like I mentioned earlier, the book of Genesis in its entirety is a most profound book. Because of the scapegoating of Joseph and his grace, mercy, and forgiveness, we essentially have an early glimpse into the entire gospel account contained within this book.

---

30. Hardin, *Jesus Driven Life*, 176.

31. See 2 Timothy 3:16.

A JOURNEY TOWARD REVELATION

The Book of Genesis is a beautiful introduction to a more peaceful Creator, but as I mentioned in chapter 1, there still remains the issue of violence attributed to God throughout the Hebrew Scriptures as a whole. A "plain" reading of scripture will never suffice as a proper hermeneutic if we are going to conclude that *God is like Jesus,* which is precisely what I attempt to do. Thus, I will introduce how I interpret Scripture, which is anthropologically first. Theology then, just as Martin Luther suggested, can begin at the cross.

I will conclude this chapter not by spending excessive time discussing the Old Testament, but by highlighting just a few of the different discussions about God found in the texts. My goal in doing this is to demonstrate how the writers of Scripture had to wrestle with the question, "Who is God?" just as we continue to do today. Whether the Psalmists are praising God,[32] or questioning his nature,[33] or whether Job is lamenting over severe scapegoating and victimization at the hands of even his closest friends[34] or yearning for the day he can finally see the one true God,[35] progress toward revelation is moving forward.[36] Girard puts it in the following way: "In the Hebrew Bible, there is clearly a dynamic that moves in the direction of the rehabilitation of the victims, but it is not a cut and dried thing. Rather it is a process under way, a text in travail; it is not a chronologically progressive process, but a struggle that advances and retreats."[37] The history of the Hebrew people begins as that of the victim. However, the oppressed eventually become the oppressors—*slaves become slave-masters.* Because of this, many views of God are presented, many different political discussions are "had," and many differ on their understanding of the expected "messiah." We cannot afford to read the Bible as if every writer agreed on matters of theology, politics, and ethics. Certainly, we must take it more seriously than to be "fundamentalist" about it.

---

32. Psalms 113–118.
33. Psalm 88.
34. Job 6.
35. Job 19:25–27
36. Hardin, *Jesus Driven Life,* 179; 184–5.
37. Hamerton-Kelly, *Violent Origins,* 141.

Henotheism

The belief in many gods was a given in the Middle Eastern region: thus, one of the more fascinating things about the Old Testament is that, although the final editors of the Hebrew Scriptures were monotheists[38], there are instances in the Old Testament that suggests some of the writers, as well as some of the Hebrew people, believed Yahweh was among a council of other gods (*elohiym*).[39] In other words, they were "henotheists"—a loose form of polytheism.[40] In the previous section, I mentioned Genesis 1:26, which states: "then God said, 'Let us make man in our image, according to our likeness . . . '" Of this phrasing, Nicholas Gier writes: "The priestly writers use singular verbs for the deity in adjacent passages; hence the use of the plural at 1:26 must be for good reason."[41] That good reason, in my opinion, is the influence of the belief in a divine council.

One such place we witness evidence of henotheism is in Deuteronomy 32:8–9, which, when sourced from the Dead Sea Scrolls, tells us:

> *When Elyon divided the nations,*
> *When he separated the sons of Adam,*
> *He established the borders of the nations*
> *According to the number of the sons of the gods.*
> *Yahweh's portion was his people,*
> *Jacob his allotted inheritance.*[42]

In both cultures (Hebrew and Babylonian) the supreme god at the point in which this was written, shares the name "El (*Elyon*)."[43] Yahweh, who was the God of the tribe of Judah, was a level under "El"—a *son* of El.[44] Another son of El was Baal, who is mentioned in such books as Judges, 1 Kings, and Numbers.[45] Yahweh was Israel's God, but he lived among other gods. In Psalm 89:6, the Psalmist rhetorically asks, "who among the heavenly beings

---

38. Gier, "Hebrew Henotheism," para. 3.

39. Ibid.

40. Henotheism is the belief in many gods. However, there is only one god worshipped within that particular religion.

41. Ibid., para. 11. See Genesis 1:27, 29–31.

42. Rabé, *Desire Found Me*, 143.

43. Ibid., 144.

44. Ibid., 141.

45. In 1 Kings 18, you will find the story of Elijah (prophet of Israel) mocking the god, Baal.

(*bên ʾēl*) is like the Lord (Yahweh)?" Obviously, no other *bên ʾēl*, or "son of El" was like Yahweh—powerful as some of the other lesser gods may have seemed at times!

In Psalm 82, we read how Yahweh becomes assimilated with El himself. The psalm, in its entirety, is as follows:

> God (elohim) has taken his place in the divine council ('adat'el);
> In the midst of the gods (elohim) he holds judgment:
> "How long will you judge unjustly
> And show partiality to the wicked? Selah
> Give justice to the weak and the needy;
> Deliver them from the hand of the wicked."
> They have neither knowledge nor understanding,
> They walk about in darkness;
> All the foundations of the earth are shaken.
> I say, "You are gods (elohim),
> Sons of the Most High, all of you;
> Nevertheless, you shall die like men,
> And fall like any prince."
> Arise, O God, judge the earth;
> For to thee belong all the nations! (RSV)

Whereas Yahweh's initial portion was only his people, in Psalm 82 "all the nations" become his. Gier responds to the "traditional" response, which denies the Jewish acknowledgment of other deities, in the following: "Traditional interpretations of this psalm have insisted that the *elohim* are really judges and not divine beings. But if the *'adat'el* is an assembly of rulers, then *elohim* in 1(b) would have no meaning. The great Ugaritic scholar Mitchel Dahood has shown the phrase *'adat'el* undoubtedly comes from the Ugaritic *'dt il*, which is the "council of El" of Canaanite mythology."[46] In my opinion, the Hebrew people declared Yahweh supreme by adapting their story to fit within the culture they came out of. When Yahweh inherits all nations, he does so after all the other gods fade away like "mortals"—falling away "like any prince" (Psalm 82:7). Only Israel's God remains to be judge over all.

Many would be hesitant to believe that the Hebrew people believed, at one point, numerous divine beings. However, ask yourself the following: Would passages such as Psalm 89:6–7 make any sense if these other gods never existed?[47] Michael Heiser contends: "How hollow it would be to have

46. Gier, "Hebrew Henotheism," para. 20.

47. Psalm 89:6–7 reads: "For who in the skies can be compared to the Lord? Who

the psalmist extolling the greatness of God by comparing him to beings which do not exist, and to in turn ask these fabricated divinities ascribe glory and strength to the Lord!"[48]

Sacrifice

A crucial aspect of all ancient religions, including that of the Jewish people, is sacrifice. One of the most appalling forms of sacrifice was that of human children.[49] There are multiple instances where child sacrifice is mentioned, but it was not just the Canaanites who performed such horrific rituals.[50] In fact, in the Book of Exodus, we have an alleged command from God concerning this. Exodus 22:29–30 states: "The firstborn of your sons you shall give to me. You shall do the same with your oxen and with your sheep . . . " Some argue away this passage by suggesting God did not demand human sacrifice because he offered a way for the child to be "redeemed" (See Exodus 13:13; 34:19–20). In other words, since God provided a satisfactory *substitute*, he never intended human sacrifice. Concerning this, Andre Rabé writes:

> If the authors thought that God did not desire human sacrifice, why not say that? The clear logic of this command is that Israel's early conception of God are that he requires human sacrifice, just as all the other tribal gods of the region. In the same manner as a substitute sacrifice can be offered for a donkey, it can be offered for the firstborn as well. If no substitute was provided for the donkey, then it had to die. If no substitute was provided for the firstborn son, he had to die. These passages do not forbid human sacrifice, they validate it.[51]

---

among the heavenly beings is like the Lord? A God feared in the council of the holy ones, great and awesome above all that are around him?"

48. Heiser, "Deuteronomy 32:8," 25.

49. In fact, the Aztecs performed child sacrifice into the sixteenth century.

50. Mesha, king of Moab, sacrifices his oldest son in 2 Kings 3:27. He does this because he was about to lose a battle against the Israelites. What should be shocking for those who hold an "inerrant" view of scripture is the verse concludes with "and there came great wrath against Israel, and they departed from him and returned to their own land." Apparently, child sacrifice to the god Kemosh worked well enough to make the Israelites flee and face "great wrath." Yet, we all now would acknowledge that Kemosh does not actually exist.

51. Rabé, *Desire Found Me*, 154.

To suggest "God commanded the child be substituted for, therefore, He never wanted the child sacrificed in the first place" simply does not follow. Yes, God provided a way for the children to be substituted for, but if he never wanted the sacrifice in the first place, just as Rabé points out, he would not have commanded such a thing. Furthermore, there are more than a few occasions where the Israelites do not exactly listen to God's commands. If someone did not follow the command to redeem their first born son (Exodus 13:13), then they were bound to offer their son as per Exodus 22:29. *Are they not?* Later writers would condemn such acts (see Jeremiah 32:35) but it seems as though at one point in their history, the Hebrew people engaged in human sacrifice.[52] I mention this not to condemn them, but to show that although they engaged in the same practices that their neighbors did, later prophets would begin to correct the Jewish understanding of God.

Although my stance that the early Israelites engaged in human sacrifice will be disputed by many, there will be no disputing that the Jewish people believed Yahweh demanded burnt offerings and sacrifice beginning prior to when he brought the Israelites out of Egypt. The first chapter of Leviticus is concerning precisely how to offer a sacrifice to God. Leviticus 1:3–5 read:

> If his offering is a burnt offering from the herd, he shall offer it, a male without defect; he shall offer it at the doorway of the tent of meeting, that he may be accepted before the Lord. He shall lay his hand on the head of the burnt offering, that it may be accepted for him to make atonement on his behalf. He shall slay the young bull before the Lord; and Aaron's sons the priests shall offer up the blood and sprinkle the blood around on the altar that is at the doorway of the tent of meeting.

While most are well aware of the fact that sacrifice is a big part of Torah, they have seemed to miss the anti-sacrificial insights some writers, such as Jeremiah, seem to have. The prophet writes:

> Add your burnt offerings to your sacrifices and eat flesh. For I (the Lord) did not speak to your fathers, or command them in the day that I brought them out of the land of Egypt, concerning burnt

52. In Judges 11:29–40, we read about Jephthah's vow to Yahweh. In this story, Jephthah promises to sacrifice the first person he sees if Yahweh grants him victory over the Ammonites. Of course, the first person Jephthah comes across after his great victory is his only daughter. Jephthah murders his daughter and there is no mention that his actions are condemned. In fact, even the writer of Hebrews includes Jephthah as one of the faithful historical figures (11:32).

offerings and sacrifices. But this is what I commanded them, saying, 'Obey My voice, and I will be your God, and you will be my
people . . . ' (Jeremiah 7:21–23)

Of course, to alleviate this potential stumbling block, the translators of the
New International Version add the word "just" in *just* the right spot. Jeremiah 7:22, in the NIV, reads: "For when I (the Lord) brought your ancestors
out of Egypt and spoke to them, I did not *just* [emphasis mine] give them
commands about burnt offerings and sacrifices. . ." Adding that little word,
which is not contained in the original Hebrew, changes the whole meaning of the passage. Did God "not give your fathers commands about burnt
offerings and sacrifices" or "not *just* give them commands about burnt offerings and sacrifices"? There is a huge difference with huge implications.
The former suggests God never wanted sacrifices while the latter suggests
he wanted sacrifice among other things.

Just as Jeremiah states that God never demanded human sacrifice (Jer.
32:35), so too in chapter 7 does it seem that God never demanded "burnt
offerings and sacrifices" of any kind. Just as the Jewish people make a move
from a belief in many gods to a belief in one God, so too do some writers
move from a god who demands blood sacrifices to one who never had it
enter his mind. We also witness this in Amos 5:21–22, where God rejects
their "festivals" and "burnt and grain offerings." I demonstrated earlier why
"festivals" that involve sacrifice and offering are reenactments of the all-
against-one violence that brought peace to the community. *Is it any wonder
God would not desire such things?*

ALL SIGNS POINT TO JESUS

The Hebrew writers certainly disagreed about various attributes of God, but
if we are willing to look closely, a trajectory away from violence and retribution and toward non-violence and grace can be seen in the scriptures. There
is a shift from henotheism, or a "council of the gods," to monotheism, where
Yahweh is "most high"—a shift from a god who demands blood for sin all
the way to a God-man who freely gives his blood for our sin. Throughout
Scripture, progressive revelation is taking place and its beautiful conclusion is the gospel revelation of Jesus Christ, who alone has authority to say,
"from now on you know him, and have seen him." (John 14:7) Marcus Borg
writes it beautifully as such:

As an epiphany of God, Jesus was a 'disclosure' or 'revelation' of God. He did not reveal God only in his teaching (as if revelation consisted primarily of information), but in his very way of being. The epiphany was Jesus—his 'person' as well as his message. As such, he was an 'image' of God, an 'icon' of God, revealing and mediating the divine reality. What he was like therefore discloses what God is like.[53]

While I feel like I covered a lot of ground in this chapter, I realize there are plenty of details anyone with the *desire* could explore further. For now, I will sum up what I have been arguing for throughout this chapter with a quote from René Girard. He writes:

What I have called 'bad sacrifice' is the kind of sacrificial religion that prevailed before Christ. It originates because mimetic rivalry threatens the very survival of a community. But through spontaneous process that also involves mimesis; the community unites against a victim in an act of spontaneous killing. This act unites rivals and restores peace and leaves a powerful impression that results in the establishment of sacrificial religion. But in this kind of religion, the community is regarded as innocent and the victim is guilty. Even after the victim has been 'deified,' he is still a criminal in the eyes of the community (. . .) but something happens that begins in the Old Testament. There are many stories that reverse this scapegoat process. In the story of Cain and Abel, the story of Joseph, the book of Job, and many of the psalms, the persecuting community is pictured as guilty and the victim is innocent. But Christ, the son of God is the ultimate 'scapegoat'—precisely because he is the son of God, and since he is innocent, he exposes all the myths of scapegoating and shows that the victims were innocent and the communities guilty.[54]

In the following chapter, I will discuss the death and resurrection of Jesus in light of what I have been arguing for throughout this chapter. Sacrifice will play a central role in how we think about Christ's death, which many, like Calvin, have strongly suggested was to assuage God's wrath. In other words, *God demanded the blood from his innocent son—the perfect sacrifice.* My goal will be to argue for a contrary, "non-violent" view of the Atonement—one that views Jesus as the truly innocent scapegoat, who

53. Borg, *Jesus A New Vision*, 191.
54. McDonald, "Violence and the Lamb Slain," para. 27.

entered into humanity's system of sacrifice, and who conquered it three days later once and for all.

5

Death and Resurrection

Rejoice greatly, O daughter Zion!
Shout aloud, O daughter Jerusalem!
Lo, your king comes to you;
Triumphant and victorious is he,
Humble and riding on a donkey.
He will cut off the chariot from Ephraim
And the war-horse from Jerusalem;
And the battle bow shall be cut off,
And he shall command peace to the nations;
His dominion shall be from sea to sea,
And from the River to the ends of the earth

Zechariah 9:9–10—NRSV

WHEN MOST CHRISTIANS VIEW the Atonement, they often take one of two stances . . . either Anselm's (1033–1109 CE) or Calvin's substitution theory. In Anselm's model, God sent Jesus to die in order to repay a great debt to satisfy God's honor. Sin is such that God's honor is greatly offended and needs blood to repay it in full. Humanity deserves wrath, but because Jesus was brutally murdered, some are saved from the slaughter before them. This differs slightly from Calvin's understanding, which agrees with the *substitution* portion but, as Calvin was a lawyer, he suggests it is an issue of "justice."

Again, presupposing God's justice as retributive, the Penal Substitution Atonement Theory emphasizes God's "wrath" (Romans 1:18)[1] toward all who have sinned (Rom. 3:23; 5:12). R.C. Sproul writes it as follows: "When the scripture tells us that God saves us, that salvation is of the Lord, we tend to forget that salvation is from the Lord."[2] In other words: Jesus saves us from God the Father. Somehow, the death of Jesus was the display of God's love, so that *some* may be saved—it was also because God demanded the blood of a perfect sacrifice (Rom. 3:25). *Jesus pays the ultimate price here on Earth to propitiate God's anger—to fulfill his demand for sacrifice—to assuage his holy vengeance.*

Because I vehemently disagree with this stance, let us look at Romans 3:25 a little closer then—*sans* a sacrificial hermeneutic. It reads: "God presented Christ as a sacrifice of atonement, through the shedding of his blood—to be received by faith. . ." (NIV) The phrase "sacrifice of atonement" is an interpretation of the Greek word *hilasterion*, which has often been translated as "propitiation" (appeasing of wrath). However, it should most accurately be translated as "mercy seat," or the "place of atonement."[3] Using a sacrificial hermeneutic, most Christians argue that the death of Jesus was a propitiation for God's wrath, rather than the place in which there is a cleansing of sin and propitiation of our wrath. Mark Heim writes:

> God enters into the position of the victim of sacrificial atonement (a position already defined by human practice) and occupies it so as to be able to act from that place to reverse sacrifice and redeem us from it. God steps forward in Jesus to be the one subject to the human practice of atonement in blood, not because that is God's preferred logic or because this itself is God's aim, but because this is the very site where human bondage and sin are enacted.[4]

---

1. I should mention this is the only verse in Romans that, in Greek, has the phrase "wrath of God." In all other instances, translators have added "of God" after "wrath" (*orge*). Regarding Romans 1:18–32 more specifically, Douglas Campbell, in his book *The Deliverance of God*, argues throughout that Paul was using a Greek rhetorical technique known as *prosopopoeia*. These verses, he argues, should be seen as a false teacher's argument, with Paul's rebuttal beginning in Romans 2. Michael Hardin makes this point: "This third view then understands the phrase 'wrath of God' to be antithetical to the gospel, but part of the false teacher's position. Following on this, all the subsequent uses of the word wrath could, if part of the rhetorical strategy, be understood as the calamity of social breakdown."—Hardin, "Guest Q & R," para. 7.

2. Sproul, R.C. *Saved from What?*, 45.

3. See Leviticus 16:16–17.

4. Heim, *Saved from Sacrifice*, 143.

Many read Romans 3:25 through the lens of sacrifice, assuming God *desired* Jesus' sacrifice for our sins. But if you take a look at how the verse begins, you should notice that it is God who offers Jesus to us. Humanity then makes the sacrifice to appease our own appetite for blood. As I demonstrated in the last chapter, sacrifice is a human construct, foundational to our religious systems and cultures. It is then all too often a projection onto God.

If we take a closer look at who is responsible for Jesus' death, and who is responsible for his life thereafter, we begin to see a clear pattern. Notice the following from the Book of Acts:[5]

2:23: *"This man (. . .) you nailed to a cross by the hands of godless men and put him to death"*	2:24: *"But God raised him up again"*
3:14—15: *"But you disowned the Holy and Righteous One and asked for a murderer to be granted to you, but put to death the Prince of life"*	3:15: *"The one whom God raised from the dead"*
4:10: *"Jesus Christ the Nazarene, whom you crucified"*	4:10: *"Whom God raised from the dead"*

Andre Rabé puts it this way: "Man does the killing and God does the making alive!"[6] God delivers the Son for us (Romans 8:32) because he does not engage in the sacred violence mankind does. Jesus opens himself to the violence mankind alone can do. Mark Heim writes:

> Jesus was already preaching the forgiveness of sins and forgiving sins before he died. He did not have to wait until after the resurrection to do that. Blood is not acceptable to God as a means of uniting human community or a price for God's favor. Christ sheds his own blood to end that way of trying to mend our divisions. Jesus' death isn't necessary because God has to have innocent blood to solve the guilt equation. Redemptive violence is our equation. Jesus didn't volunteer to get into God's justice machine. God volunteered to get into ours. God used our own sin to save us.[7]

My goal is not to spend too long on Penal Substitution Theory or any substitutionary understanding of the cross because, frankly, they all presuppose God's demand for *sacrifice*. To interpret through this sacrificial lens is

5. Table sourced from Rabe, *Desire Found Me*, 224.

6. Ibid.

7. Heim, *Saved from Sacrifice*, xi.

to view things as they have always been since the development of religion itself. If you will recall, in chapter 4, I discuss how Cain and Abel present offerings to God prior to any mention that He wanted them in the first place—*this is just what humans do!* It seems the great majority of Christianity cannot keep herself from thinking God demands something in order to give something. In spite of the anti-sacrificial passages from Jeremiah 7, Amos 5, Psalm 40 and, as I will point out in the following chapter, much of the New Testament, the sacrificial lens remains the mainstream.

Throughout the remainder of this chapter, I will build upon what I began primarily in the last. The conclusion to the story will be the death and resurrection of our Lord, Jesus Christ. I hope to present an understanding of this universe-changing event that places the guilt of violence squarely where it belongs—on the shoulders of humanity. Yet, in spite of such dehumanizing violence, Christ returns with the word of peace—*shalom*.[8]

ESCALATING HOSTILITY

In the previous chapter, I introduced mimetic theory and its various components. During the scapegoating process, I discussed how a mob forms and how the all against all violence transforms into all against one. The gospel story is one such story where this occurs. Only this time, the scapegoat is the Son of God . . . but he will speak a better word than Abel.[9]

Because Jesus lived under the rule of the Roman Empire, it was only inevitable that he was going to come up against their brute force. He was performing signs and healing others (John 9:1–7) and warning the "scribes and Pharisees" about their violence and persecution. As we have now witnessed over and over throughout history, going up against the religious and political authorities is a key ingredient for your own persecution and bloodshed. Notice the tone Jesus takes in Matthew 23:29–35. The passage reads:

> Woe to you, scribes and Pharisees, hypocrites! For you build the tombs of the prophets and adorn the monuments of the righteous, and say, 'If we had been living in the days of our fathers, we would not have been partners with them in shedding the blood of the prophets.' So you testify against yourselves, that you are sons of those who murdered the prophets. Fill up, then, the measure of the

8. *Shalom* is the Hebrew word for "peace."

9. Hebrews 12:24—more on this verse in the third section of this chapter.

guilt of your fathers. You serpents, you brood of vipers, how will you escape the sentence of hell?[10] Therefore, behold, I am sending you prophets and wise men and scribes; some of them you will kill and crucify, and some of them you will scourge in your synagogues, and persecute from city to city, so that upon you may fall the guilt of all the righteous blood shed on earth, from the blood of righteous Abel to the blood of Zechariah, the son of Berechiah, whom you murdered between the temple and the altar.

By pointing out the Pharisee's hypocrisy and by including them in sacred violence, Jesus is putting himself in the crosshairs of their soon to be out of control contempt and rage.

As I demonstrated in the previous chapter, civilizations are founded on a murder.[11] The first city in the Bible, *founded* after the murder of Abel, is no exception. The final murder in the Old Testament is that of Zechariah, found in 2 Chronicles 24: 20–21.[12] The Old Testament is bookended with murder—innocent blood. Jesus' actions in Matthew 23 make his own death imminent. In fact, Christ expands that by correctly prophesying that there will be prophets sent that will share in his fate—adding to the growing list of victims the religious authorities have brutally murdered.[13] In John 11, Jesus' fate becomes sealed.

After Jesus raises Lazarus, the people are divided—some to believe in him, yet others to rat him out to the Pharisees. John 11: 47–53 reads:

Therefore the chief priests and the Pharisees convened a council, and were saying, 'What are we doing? For this man is performing many signs. If we let him go on like this, all men will believe in him, and the Romans will come and take away both our place and our nation.' But one of them, Caiaphas, who was high priest that year, said to them, 'You know nothing at all, nor do you take into account that it is expedient for you that one man die for the people, and that the whole nation not perish.' Now he did not say this on his own initiative, but being high priest that year, he prophesied that Jesus was going to die for the nation, and not for the nation only, but in order that He might also gather together into one the

---

10. Gehenna.

11. See also, the myth as to how the Greek city of Thebes is founded. In this tale, Cadmus uses the teeth of a slain dragon to create an army of warriors. He then causes the men to die until only five are left. Those five men then begin to construct the city.

12. Hardin, *Jesus Driven Life*, 105.

13. Ibid.

children of God who are scattered abroad. So from that day on they planned together to kill him.

Notice how Jesus' sacrificial death will save not only "the nation," but will "also gather together into one the children of God who are scattered abroad." As I discussed in chapter 4, the scapegoat is the cause of the problems of the community in the first place (John 11:48) and once destroyed, the bringer of peace (John 11:50—51).

As I will discuss in chapter 8, the Romans indeed take all that the Jewish people had in 70 CE. However, it will not be due to the scapegoated victim, but due to their insistence in dealing with their enemies, specifically the Romans, with violence. Placing the preemptive blame of their eventual fall on Jesus is the beginning of the single victim mechanism—where *all will turn against one to save all.* The Pharisees are blind to what is directly in front of them; blind to the sacred violence they are engaging in. But, the decision has been made—the cause of their problems, the one who will lead to their ruin—will bring peace and save them all, if only he be destroyed.

GUILTY!

In spite of what was certainly in front of him, Jesus enters Jerusalem in the fashion described in Zechariah 9. He enters on a "young donkey," saying "fear not, daughter of Zion; behold, your King is coming, seated on a donkey's colt" (John 12:15). This King is the one who comes to "cut off the chariots . . . the war horse . . . and the bow of war."[14]

There are instances where Jesus could have stopped his torturous death. In the Garden of Gethsemane, he could have unleashed "legions of angels" on his captors.[15] Yet, he does not—*why?* First, the Son of Man came to expose our sacrificial system, our sacred violence, our scapegoating. To expose these systems, he must take non-violence to its finality. Second in doing so, he also reveals the nature of his Father, which is rooted in his perfect and unconditional love. Jesus "can only do what he sees his Father doing, because whatever the Father does the Son does also" (John 5:19—NIV). Focusing my attention back on the substitution model, I cannot help but wonder: If Jesus is a substitutionary sacrifice to assuage God's

14. See Zechariah 9:10.
15. See Matthew 26:53.

retributive punishment, is Jesus, *in doing only what the Father does*, sacrificing himself? I think not! He does, however, enter Jerusalem and allow us to.

Once Jesus is betrayed, a key ingredient to any single-victim mechanism is used in order to convict this *blasphemer*—gossip. Matthew 26:59 reads: "Now the chief priests and the whole council kept trying to obtain *false testimony* [emphasis mine] against Jesus, so that they might put him to death." By verse 65, violence begins and an angry mob is born. The high priest and others from the council begin to beat Jesus. Once in front of Governor Pilate, it is only a matter of time until the most infamous murder in the history of mankind unfolds. Shortly, Pilate will have no choice but to convict Jesus. Matthew 27: 21–26 tells us:

> The governor said to them, 'which of the two do you want me to release for you?' And they said, 'Barabbas.' Pilate said to them, 'then what shall I do with Jesus who is called Christ?' They all said, 'Crucify him!' And he said, 'Why, what evil has he done?' But they kept shouting all the more, saying, 'Crucify him!' When Pilate saw that he was accomplishing nothing, but rather that a riot was starting, he took water and washed his hands in front of the crowd, saying, 'I am innocent of this man's blood, see to that yourselves.' And all the people said, 'his blood shall be on us and on our children!' Then he released Barabbas for them; but after having Jesus scourged, he handed him over to be crucified.

Pilate is damned if he does and damned if he doesn't. An angry mob had already developed and blood was going to be spilled—either Jesus' or, if things got too out-of-hand, Pilate's. At minimum, his governorship would certainly be lost. *Should we have really expected the governor of a Roman province to allow a riot to ensue because of his softness toward some Jewish prophet?* A Roman politician, no matter how much he may desire to save Jesus, was no match for the power of the angry lynch mob.

All manners of evil become front and center during the death of Jesus. Whereas, in Jewish practice, the atoning blood sacrifice is performed in the most sacred of places, the Holy of Holies; the sacrifice of the atoning blood of Jesus was spilled in the most profane of places—*right in public*. Michael Hardin writes:

> The difference between Jesus' death and that of the prophets, from Abel to Zechariah, was that their deaths took place in or by sacred altars; it was in the context of sacrifice, near a bloody altar that they die. Jesus does not die in the Temple or near the altar. His

death is completely secularized; he dies on a hill 'outside the city gate' (Hebrews 13:12).[16]

Jesus is mocked (Matthew 27:27–32) and then crucified in the most gruesome of manners for all to see. And in the midst of this, I would like to point out two important things. First, there is a Roman centurion who admits "truly this was the Son of God!"[17] When this happens, any supposed guilt of the victim—the scapegoat—is exposed as *false*. Paul states that Jesus "made a public display of them" (Colossians 2:15). No amount of horror, violence, wrath, anger, or vengeance could manipulate Jesus. Because of this, for the first time, the guilty party can plainly witness their guilt. It is on full display—out in the open—for the world to see! Second, the Christ who will be "lifted up as Lord,"[18] in the midst of *everything* states "Father, forgive them; for they do not know what they are doing" (Luke 23:34). *Remember: Jesus only does what he sees his Father doing.* All Jesus desired to do was offer forgiveness, because that is all he must have seen from his Father. As Paul puts it, he forgives us "while we were yet sinners" (Romans 5:8).

RESURRECTION, MERCY, AND PEACE

After Jesus' death, all must have seemed lost to those who believed he was their messiah—their savior. *Empire wins again, just like they always do.* How could Jesus be the messiah if he was dead? *He certainly did not live up to the promise that he would deliver Israel.* However, it is not long until the extraordinary happens—Mary Magdalene and others encounter the Risen Christ.[19] Certainly, in the minds of Second Temple Jews, *now* God was going to bring hell-fire and retribution considering humanity had just killed his son. However, notice how Jesus approaches his disciples. John 20:19–23 reads:

> So when it was evening on that day, the first day of the week, and when the doors were shut where the disciples were, for fear of the Jews, Jesus came and stood in their midst and said to them, 'Peace be with you.' And when he had said this, he showed them both his hands and his side. The disciples then rejoiced when they saw

16. Hardin, *Jesus Driven Life*, 105.

17. See Matthew 27:54.

18. When it is said that Jesus is exalted on a cross, even the language that is used is a subversion of how a king is generally exalted by the people.

19. See John 20:11–17; Luke 24:13–27.

the Lord. So Jesus said to them again, 'Peace be with you; as the Father has sent me, I also send you.' And when he had said this, he breathed on them and said to them, 'Receive the Holy Spirit. If you forgive the sins of any, their sins have been forgiven them; if you retain the sins of any, they have been retained.'

Jesus forgave during his own murder and brings the message of peace and forgiveness to his disciples after his resurrection. *No retribution or vengeance—just peace and forgiveness.* Where the blood of Abel cried out for vengeance, the blood of Jesus, in contrast, speaks a far better word—peace (Hebrews 12:24).

He then gives his disciples the most wonderful of blessings—the Holy Spirit—and instructs them to forgive as he forgives (v. 21). In perfect imitation, Jesus gives to his disciples what the Father gave him. James Alison illustrates this with his coined phrase, "the intelligence of the victim":

What links the Father and Jesus, therefore, is the intelligence of the victim. It is in the light of the intelligence of the victim that we can begin to understand the relationship between the two— the love for us that involved sending Jesus, the love for Jesus that involved sending, and raising him up, the love which Jesus had for his Father which involved giving himself for us knowingly to victimization. It is this knowledge of the intelligence of the victim which sets us free: the truth which sets us free is the truth of the victim. The Counselor [*Paraclete*], the Spirit of truth, who is the advocate for the defense against the lynching of the world, this is the intelligence of the victim, bearing witness to the truth which flows from the victim (. . .) the Holy Spirit is the intelligence of the victim.[20]

Our Mirror

When Jesus returns all the violence humanity can throw at him with forgiveness, he shows us who the Father is and what we are to be like. We are shown the way out of our continual cycle of bloodshed, violence, and madness. Andre Rabé beautifully sums this up in the following:

The message of Jesus breaks this cycle of evil by giving us a new reference for who we are. The victim is no longer a victim if he or she chooses forgiveness instead of revenge. The victimizer no

20. Alison, *Knowing Jesus*, 112–13.

longer needs to live in the shame of his or her evil as they receive forgiveness. Jesus introduces us to our true mirror—the God in whose image and likeness we were created to reflect dignity, love and the courage to be our true selves even in the midst of a perverse world.[21]

When Jesus offers this radical forgiveness, he is displaying love in its fullest form. Jesus refuses to condemn his victimizers and as followers, it becomes strikingly self-evident that this is to be mirrored. Jesus mirrors the Father, models for us the spirit of forgiveness and peace, and we are to mirror this to bring about true healing in a world desperate for it. This type of love—the miracle that it is—is what sets all free. We are free from the need to accuse or condemn—free to love as Jesus loves us. I love how Michael Hardin describes this in the following:

> It is our encounter with the Vindicated Victim who forgives us and restores our relation to God that is the basis for the new imitation. We are still creatures of imitation even after we have been forgiven and reconciled so it stands to reason that we will also continue to imitate, but in the encounter with the Risen Lord, we are given choice for the first time. We can either continue to imitate each other and end up again and again before the cross with our victims, or we can now choose to imitate Jesus. It is not the historical Jesus we imitate, it is the living Lord.[22]

In the following, I will explain why the resurrection event offers hope to all. Although death in this life may seem like the end, it most certainly is not the final word for our Father has much more in store for us.

Why the Resurrection?

As I mentioned in chapter 4, all civilizations throughout history are founded upon murder—a tomb and a dead body. However, because of the resurrection of the one in whom we place our hope, Christian community, which I will discuss in chapter 9, is founded upon the empty tomb of Jesus.

Notice that when Jesus reveals himself to the disciples, he carries with him the scars of the violence he endured. His hands and side are even felt and seen by an unbelieving Thomas. However, his body has been healed and is no longer kept in a tomb to decompose and rot—he is present with

21. Rabé, *Desire Found Me*, 228.

22. Hardin, *Jesus Driven Life*, 145.

them. He comes back as the victim—wounded yet forgiving; battered but healed. It is as if Jesus is saying, "As I told you all before, my body is for you—to be broken by you. An in spite of that, I come back healed and offering peace to you." In order to deliver the postmortem message of forgiveness, he had to be resurrected. His scars bear the proof of his victimage, but his words of peace bear witness to the Father's commitment to forgiveness and non-violence.

In giving himself freely for all, Jesus opened himself up to all manners of evil. He entered into the satanic ritualistic practice of sacrifice and in his slaying, exposed it. However, the resurrection tells us that death is not the end of the story. Because Jesus was resurrected, so too will those he died for—we have a promise that what Jesus did worked for him, so it will work for us. This modeling opens up the freedom for us to forgive even those who would take our life. The resurrection states God has the final answer and that answer is forgiveness, peace, and life everlasting.

CONCLUDING REMARKS

In this chapter, I attempted to make the case for a non-violent atonement—or, a mimetic "*at-one-ment.*" In other words, Jesus allows himself to be a sacrifice to propitiate humanity's wrath, becoming our model as we "follow him." Jesus thought himself nothing to be grasped at. He was content with his full humanness, even to the point of suffering on the cross. He does this because so too does his Father. When we suffer, God suffers. Jürgen Moltmann writes:

> If God were incapable of suffering in every aspect, then he would also be incapable of love. He would at most be capable of loving himself, but not of loving another as himself, as Aristotle puts it. But if he is capable of loving something else, then he lays himself open to the suffering which love for another brings him; and yet, by virtue of his love, he remains master of the pain that love causes him to suffer. God does not suffer out of deficiency of being, like created beings (. . .) but he suffers from the love which is the superabundance and overflowing of his being.[23]

In the forgiveness of the systemic sin that nailed his Son to a Roman cross is where both God's love and his suffering are the fullest. Because of our wrath, Jesus had to be humiliated in the most profane of spaces and endured

23. Moltmann, *Trinity and the Kingdom*, 23.

it all. God was willing to give up his cherished and beloved Son in order to save his creation. At the cross is where we meet our Abba who accepts our systems of violence and conquers them.

Throughout the last two chapters, I only scratched the surface with regards to mimetic theory and a non-violent atonement. My intention was to offer a succinct, yet thorough explanation as to how one takes a Christo-centric hermeneutic, or "Christ-centered interpretation of the Bible." In the following chapter, I will piggyback on this and discuss how both Jesus and Paul quoted the Hebrew Scriptures; pointing to multiple instances where any vengeance associated to God is omitted.

6

Scripture's Internal Hermeneutic

IN THE PREVIOUS CHAPTER, I demonstrated that Jesus came and offered himself to us, propitiating our wrath, not his Father's. The death of Jesus is the culmination of the journey in how we came to understand the nature of God. In this chapter, piggybacking on the previous two, I will point to multiple instances, whether in the Gospel of Luke, the Epistle to the Hebrews, or Paul's letter to the Galatians, where we can witness a specific "internal hermeneutic" that leads us away from understanding God as violent and retributive. Note: *You should have a Bible handy throughout this chapter.*

As I have mentioned on numerous occasions, a *prima facie* reading of Scripture can lead to any number of conclusions; too often leading to understandings of Christ's mission and message that I find extremely far-fetched and off-base. If we are going to "follow" Jesus as he commands in Matthew 4:19, we must take him seriously enough to view him *not only* as divine, but also as fully human—a Jewish Rabbi who lived in and amongst a people in occupied Israel/Palestine. We do this precisely because that is the context in which he lived and taught. He used language his people would understand, spoke to various people within the framework of their own culture, and lived a very real existence in a very human way. If we fail to recognize this, we end up having the version of Christianity we have today—where thousands of contradictory versions of Jesus exist.

One such way in which many draw incorrect understandings is by believing the Old Testament is the context of the New. However, that belief needs to be replaced by one that recognizes that Second Temple Judaism is the context in which we view the synoptic gospels[1], the fourth gospel (John's), and the Apostle Paul. After all, there is roughly a 500 year gap between the final book of the Old Testament (Malachi) and Matthew's Gospel.

THE HERMENEUTICS OF JESUS

While some Christians contend that (1) there was Scripture in Jesus' day, and (2) He quoted from said Scripture, it follows that (3) *He accepted its authority in its entirety.* First, this begs the question as to what is to be considered scripture. Not all Jewish groups agreed on which texts were authoritative and which were not.[2] Which books did Jesus deem authoritative? Was the Book of Jubilees authoritative? How about I Enoch? Notice in the short Epistle of Jude, found in the New Testament, Jude quotes the book of 1 Enoch, which is not considered canon by most Western Christian denominations. Take a look at the comparison between 1 Enoch 1:9 and Jude 14 –15 below.

I Enoch 1:9: *"And behold! He cometh with ten thousands of His Saints to execute judgment upon all, and to destroy all the ungodly: and to convict all flesh of all the works of their ungodliness which they have ungodly committed, and of all the hard things which ungodly sinners have spoken against Him."*	Jude 14–15: *"'It was also about these men that Enoch, in the seventh generation from Adam, prophesied, saying, 'Behold, the Lord came with many thousands of His holy ones, to execute judgment upon all, and to convict all the ungodly of all their ungodly deeds which they have done in an ungodly way, and of all the harsh things which ungodly sinners have spoken against Him.'"*

Certainly, it appears as if Jude thought 1 Enoch to be authoritative, yet we today would not. At least, no Christian I have ever met carried around the book of 1 Enoch with them. And further yet, how should we define "authoritative"? Is anything but a literal, fundamentalist reading of Scripture contradictory to what "authoritative" should be defined as? Does the Bible have to be viewed as the Word of God, where every little detail is an axiomatic truth from God, or all authority is lost? If these questions are affirmed then, all-too-often, Jesus seems nowhere to be found.

In this section, I hope to demonstrate how Jesus read Scripture quite dissimilarly to how most Christians read it now. Where Jesus had a specific

---

1. The gospels of Matthew, Mark, and Luke.

2. Hardin, "Reading the Bible from a Peacemaking Perspective," part 4.

hermeneutic that subverted his Father's alleged violence, Western Christians too-often employ a hermeneutic that adds violence back into the equation. I believe, rather than pigeonholing himself to fit existing Scripture, Jesus models how to creatively read it in light of his peaceful mission.

Jesus' "Magnum Opus"

The most compelling instance where Jesus employs a "creative" reading of Jewish Scripture is during the *Sermon on the Mount,* found in the Matthew's Gospel. After Jesus commands Peter, Andrew, James, and John to follow him,[3] Christ, in similar, but not exact fashion to Moses[4] heads up into the mountain to declare the commandments of God to the people (Matthew 5:1). It is in that sermon in which Jesus gives his most famous and quoted teachings. On several occasions, he begins a sentence with "you have heard that it was said"; but then offers a new teaching by uttering; "but I say to you." In the following table, I will list each instance in which Jesus seems to be redefining what is expected of "God's people."

"You have heard that it was said" / "You have heard that the ancients were told"	*"But I say to you"*
v. 21: "You shall not commit murder"[A]	v. 22: "Everyone who is angry with his brother shall be guilty before the court"
v. 27: "You shall not commit adultery"[B]	v. 28: "Everyone who looks at a woman with lust for her has already committed adultery with her in his heart"
v. 31: "Whoever sends his wife away, let him give her a certificate of divorce"[C]	v. 32: "Everyone who divorces his wife, except for the reason of unchastity, makes her commit adultery; and whoever marries a divorced woman commits adultery"
v. 33: "You shall not make false vows, but shall fulfill your vows to the Lord"[D]	v. 34: "Make no oath at all"
v. 38: "An eye for an eye"[E]	v. 39: "Do not resist an evil person; but whoever slaps you on your right cheek, turn the other to him also"
v. 43: "You shall love your neighbor and hate your enemy"[F]	v. 44: "Love your enemies and pray for those who persecute you"

3. See Matthew 4: 18–22.

4. See Exodus 19–20

A. Exodus 20:13.

B. See Exodus 20:14.

C. See Deuteronomy 24:1.

D. See Ecclesiastes 5:4; Numbers 30:1–2.

E. See Leviticus 24:20.

F. The first clause is from Leviticus 19:18 and the second is an overall view the Israelites had about their "enemies."

The goal of the Law is peace. Thus, Jesus finds no reason to abolish it. He states: "do not think that I came to abolish the Law of the Prophets; I did not come to abolish but to fulfill" (Matthew 5:17). He fulfills it by modeling how true peace is achieved—by being non-retributive like the Father. Girard explains this in the following:

> When Jesus declares that he does not abolish the Law but fulfills it, he articulates a logical consequence of his teaching. The goal of the Law is peace among humankind. Jesus never scorns the Law, even when it takes the form of prohibitions. Unlike modern thinkers, he knows quite well that to avoid conflicts, it is necessary to begin with prohibitions.[5]

Jesus instructs: where once there was an "economy of exchange" (adhere to X law, or Y consequence will occur), now there is love for all, including our enemies. Because this is the crux of his commandments, I want to focus on the verses that speak to such a command; namely verses 43–45. They read: "You have heard that it was said, 'you shall love your neighbor and hate your enemy.' But I say to you, love your enemies and pray for those who persecute you, so that you may be sons of your Father who is in heaven; for he causes his sun to rise on the evil and the good, and sends rain on the righteous and the unrighteous." As I will discuss at length in the following section, Jesus seems keen on introducing something that is completely foreign to the Jewish people. In fact, what Jesus is teaching seems to be a *direct contradiction* of Proverbs 3:33, which states: "The curse of the Lord is on the house of the wicked, but he blesses the dwelling of the righteous." So which is it? Does God send "rain on the righteous *and* unrighteous," or put the wicked under a "curse"?

This must have been difficult for Second Temple Jews to hear! For the first time, the followers of God are instructed to "turn the other cheek," forever disavowing a retributivist mindset. *Why?* If you notice how the sermon concludes in Matthew 5, you read all of the new teachings leading

5. Girard, *I See Satan*, 14.

up to the final verse of the chapter, which reads: "therefore, you are to be perfect, as your heavenly Father is perfect" (5:48). The Father is everything Christ taught in Matthew 5: loving those who are difficult to love (5:44) and returning evil with good (5:39–42). No longer is God to be thought of as a God who takes sides (Israel's), for he also blesses both "the righteous and the unrighteous" (5:45). Whereas, in chapter 5, I discussed the actions of Jesus that are to be mirrored, the Sermon on the Mount is the "instructions" on how to start thinking about God. Jesus models precisely how to imitate the Father both in lesson and in action.

In this sermon, he begins to draw a conclusion, so to speak, to the question, "Who is God?" the Hebrew people had been exploring throughout their history. Their understanding of the divine takes many twists and turns, but, revelation takes place during the Sermon on the Mount.

"And the day of Vengeance of our God"

A powerful illustration in which Jesus quotes The Old Testament quite selectively can be found in Luke 4. After having been baptized and tested in the wilderness, Jesus returns to Galilee "in the power of the Spirit" (4:14). Once in the synagogue of his hometown, Jesus begins to read from the book of Isaiah. In the following table, I will parallel the two passages; namely Luke 4:18–19 and Isaiah 61:1–2.

Luke 4:18–19	Isaiah 61:1–2
Jesus: "The Spirit of the Lord is upon me, because he anointed me to preach the gospel to the poor. He has sent me to proclaim release to the captives, and recovery of sight to the blind, to set free those who are oppressed, to proclaim the favorable year of the Lord."	"The Spirit of the Lord God is upon me, Because the Lord has anointed me To bring good news to the afflicted; He has sent me to bind up the brokenhearted, To proclaim liberty to captives And freedom to prisoners; To proclaim the favorable year of the Lord *And the day of vengeance of our God* [emphasis mine]."

The detail to notice is that Jesus leaves off the last line from Isaiah 61:2, specifically; "*and the day of vengeance of our God.*" By doing this, he is again redefining the Israelites' understanding of the Father. Shortly after closing the scroll, Jesus concludes his brief reading with: "Today this Scripture has been fulfilled in your hearing" (4:21). In other words, Jesus is telling the

Galilean listeners that he is the one fulfilling the prophecy about the coming messiah.

Jesus' listeners were so enraged by what he was teaching that "they got up and drove him out of the city, and led him to the brow of a hill on which their city had been built, in order to throw him down the cliff" (4:29). Why? I trust it is because they noticed how Jesus was subverting attributes of the very God they worshiped. In their minds, if God was not retributive, seeking vengeance on the enemies of Israel, then they would never be free from their oppressors (i.e., the Roman Empire).[6] However, there still remains one short phrase in verse 22 that creates a potential stumbling block in this interpretation of the story.

In *The Jesus Driven Life*, Michael Hardin sheds much needed light on the proper manner in which to interpret what takes place between the conclusion of Jesus' reading and his attempted murder. Shortly after Jesus concludes his message in 4:21, verse 22 tells us that "*all were speaking well of Him* [emphasis mine], and wondering at the gracious words which were falling from His lips; and they were saying, 'is this not Joseph's son?'" The original Greek text should have been properly translated as "and all bore witness (*emartyroun autō*) to him," rather than "all were speaking well of him."[7] The Greek phrase, "*emartyroun autō*," does not carry a positive or negative connotation but translators have decided to translate it *positively*, causing later verses not to seem to follow naturally.[8] More appropriately, the phrase "bore witness" should be rendered as a "statement of disadvantage."[9] In other words, Jesus' listeners "witnessed against" him.

Why would Galileans—Second Temple Jews—waiting for God to deliver the people of Israel from their oppressors, "speak well of" Jesus after he blatantly omitted the text that spoke to the only thing that could deliver them; namely, Yahweh's vengeance? *In short, they would not!* Furthermore, if the listeners were indeed "speaking well of him," it does not follow that Jesus would start antagonizing them by saying "no prophet is welcome in his hometown" (4:24) and by pointing out that two of Israel's prophets, Elijah and Elisha, worked miracles among the enemies of Israel (4:25–27) and

---

6. The Roman Empire took control of Palestine in 63 BCE and had to administratively reorganize when Judaea became part of the province of Syria-Palestine around 132–135 CE.

7. Hardin, *Jesus Driven Life*. 61.

8. Ibid.

9. Hardin, "Reading the Bible from a Peacemaking Perspective," part 4.

thus, to an ordinary Second Temple Jew, the enemies of God.[10] It would follow more logically that Jesus was responding to the listeners' sarcasm and negativity, due to the absence of the text in Isaiah that speaks to God's "vengeance," than the reverse.[11]

Fill them with Corpses?

Another instance where Jesus employs a creative exegesis of Scripture and then eliminates the vengeance of the Father is found in Matthew 22:42–45, Mark 12:35–40, and Luke 20:41–47.[12] In all three accounts, Jesus is quoting from Psalm 110, which is the most quoted Hebrew text found in the New Testament.[13] Psalm 110, in its entirety, reads:

The Lord says to my Lord:
'Sit at My right hand
Until I make your enemies a footstool for your feet.'
The Lord will stretch forth your strong scepter from Zion, saying,
'Rule in the midst of your enemies.'
Your people will volunteer freely in the day of your power;
In holy array, from the womb of the dawn,
Your youth are to you as the dew.
The Lord has sworn and will not change his mind,
'You are a priest forever
According to the order of Melchizedek.'
The Lord is at your right hand;
He will shatter kings in the day of his wrath.
He will judge among the nations,
He will fill them with corpses,
He will shatter the chief men over a broad country.
He will drink from the brook by the wayside;
Therefore he will lift up his head."

What is interesting is that in all three instances, just prior to quoting the text from Psalms, Jesus adds the phrase; "David himself said." Luke 20:41–44 reads: "Then he said to them, 'How is it that they say the Christ is David's son? For David himself says in the book of the Psalms, 'The Lord said to my

10. Ibid., 62.

11. Ibid., 60.

12. Three different accounts of the same event.

13. Ibid., 135. There are twenty-five New Testament instances where Psalm 110 is referenced.

Lord, sit at my right hand, until I make your enemies a footstool for your feet.' Therefore David calls him 'Lord,' and how is he his son?" Peter Enns explains what Jesus is doing in the passage above:

> In its ancient Israelite context, the psalmist is speaking the first part and simply announcing what God is saying to his (the psalmist's) king, either David or a king in David's line, hence: The Lord (God) says to my lord (David/descendent) followed by what God says to this king (the quoted portion). But Jesus reads the psalm differently. He takes the beginning of the psalm as coming from David himself (not the psalmist writing about David). So now you have David referring to one of his descendents as "my lord," and so Psalm 110 in Jesus' hands becomes a proof text "prediction" about Jesus.[14]

In other words, the original context was for the *first Lord to be interpreted as God*, and the *second lord as David or one of David's descendent*. However, Jesus interpreted the psalm as the *first "Lord" being God* while the *second lord was Jesus, a descendent of David—yet referred by David as "lord."* Hardin contends Christ is saying something ironically, to the effect of "your Bible says this and since you believe your Bible is inspired you must answer the question."[15]

In addition to this "creative" reading of Scripture, he then eliminates the verses that speak of God's violence and wrath (vv. 2–3, 5–7).[16] In doing so, he is reshaping his listeners' understanding of "messiah"; which must be done because of all of the erroneous presupposed understandings about who the messiah was going to be. Enns writes: "A popular belief of the day among some Jews was that God would one day send a king from the line of David, a 'messiah' who would deliver the Jews from their present state as tenants in their own land under Roman authority."[17] From henceforth, according to the testimony of Jesus, "messiah" should not be synonymous with "militant deliverer," as Michael Hardin puts it, but as a peaceful lamb. Hardin asserts: "I would say that verses 2–3 and 5–6 are omitted in the New Testament discussion of Jesus' messiahship because they participate in the sacrificial reading, a way of thinking I believe Jesus intentionally sought to

---

14. Enns, "Jesus Didn't Read His Bible Like We Do," para. 9.

15. Hardin, "Reading the Bible from a Peacemaking Perspective," Part 3.

16. Ibid.

17. Ibid., See 2 Samuel 7.

expose."[18] Furthermore, it behooves me to point out that *nowhere* in the New Testament are the "retributive" verses of Psalm 110 ever quoted. Even when verses 1 and 4 are referenced together, such as in Hebrews 5:6, 6:20, 7:17, and 7:21, no mention of Psalm 110: 2–3; 5–6 can be found.[19]

"Blessed is he. . ."

> The disciples of John reported to him about all these things. Summoning two of his disciples, John sent them to the Lord, saying, 'are you the expected One, or do we look for someone else?' When the men came to him, they said, 'John the Baptist has sent us to you, to ask, 'are you the expected One, or do we look for someone else?" At that very time he cured many people of diseases and afflictions and evil spirits; and he gave sight to many who were blind. And he answered and said to them, 'go and report to John what you have seen and heard: the blind receive sight, the lame walk, the lepers are cleansed, and the deaf hear, the dead are raised up, the poor have the Gospel preached to them. Blessed is he who does not take offense at me.' (Luke 7:18–23)

To give you a little back-story to the passage above: Jesus is speaking to the "disciples of John," who believed God was vengeful and would bring about the destruction of the enemies of Israel.[20] Luke 3:7 tells us: "So he (John) began saying to the crowds who were going out to be baptized by him, 'you brood of vipers, who warned you to flee from the wrath to come?'" Now, Jesus, in telling John of the various miracles he has been performing, is not telling the "baptizer," who is in prison at the time, anything he does not know already.[21] What Jesus *is* doing is apparently causing a scandal (7:23), one that caused John quite a good deal of torment. In quot-

---

18. Hardin, *Jesus Driven Life*, 135.

19. Comparisons of Jesus to the high priest Melchizedek of Psalm 110:4 are only found in the epistle to the Hebrews. Melchizedek's role, according to the *Dead Sea Scroll* fragment 11QMelch, is to restore Israel to a righteous state through the use of vengeance. However, because Melchizedek was known as the "king of righteousness" and "king of peace"; and because the violent verses of Psalm 110 are omitted in every reference found in the New Testament, with Christ as the high priest (forever, according to the order of Melchizedek (110:4)), no such vengeance applies. Thus, Psalm 110: 2–3; 5–7 are never mentioned in any references in either the synoptic gospels or the Epistle to the Hebrews. See Swartley, *Covenant of Peace*, 255 and Hardin, *Jesus Driven Life*, Appendix A for more.

20. Hardin, *Jesus Driven Life*, 63.

21. Ibid.

ing various Hebrew texts (primarily Isaianic) that prophesy of his coming
(as I will display in the following table), Jesus yet again omits all associated
"vengeance passages."[22]

Miracle of Jesus	Old Testament Reference	Associated Vengeance Found In. . .
Sight to the blind	Isa. 61:1–2; 29:18; 35:5	Isa. 61:2 Isa. 29:20; Isa. 35:4
The lame to walk	Isa. 35:6	Isa. 35:4
The deaf to hear	Isa. 29:18; 35:5	Isa. 29:20; 35:4
Preach the Gospel to the poor	Isa. 29:19	Isa. 29:20
Cleanse lepers/raise the dead	1 Kings 17:17–24; 2 Kings 5:1–27	

After omitting all the associated "vengeance" passages, Jesus then concludes his brief message with *"blessed is he who does not take offense at me"*
(v. 23). Certainly, considering John's quote in Luke 3:7, coupled with the
fact that he was already well aware of the miracles Jesus had been performing, any "offense" that could be taken would have been Christ's omission of
vengeance attributed to the Father.

ACCORDING TO THE LAW

In the previous section, I pointed to several occasions in which Jesus employed a creative reading of Scripture; always eliminating retributive violence associated with the Father. In this section, I will argue that the very
same thing is done *vis-à-vis* the Law of Torah.

Some may point to Hebrews 9:22 to "prove" that God requires, or at
least at some point in time required, blood to be spilt in order for forgiveness to ensue. It is also a favorite "proof-text" to argue in favor of Penal
Substitution Atonement Theory. Verse 22 reads: "And according to the Law,
one may almost say, all things are cleansed with blood, and without shedding of blood there is no forgiveness." The important thing to notice about
this verse is that it is the *Law—which is already under indictment in the
earlier chapters of this epistle (7:18 and 8:13 in particular)—* that requires
cleansing with blood. In Hebrews 10:5–7, exegeting from Psalm 40: 6–8,
the sacrificial components of *Law* get completely turned-on-their-head in

22. Table sourced from Ibid.

the following: "Sacrifice and offering you did not desire, but a body you prepared for me; with burnt offerings and sin offerings you were not pleased. Then I said, 'Here I am—it is written about me in the scroll—I have come to do your will, my God.'" According to this passage, and piggybacking on what Jeremiah stated (Jeremiah 7:23—see chapter 4), the sacrificial aspect of the Law was not a desire of God's (10:5), nor was it pleasing (10:6). In fact, verse 8 suggests God did not desire, nor was he pleased, with sacrifice, *even though* they are "offered according to the Law." *So which is it?* Did God dictate the sacrificial aspects of Levitical Law, as a more "literal" reading would suggest, or, am I misinterpreting Jeremiah and the writer of Hebrews? Is God a god who demands sacrifice or, as I believe, did not desire it *even though* it was such an important part of the Jewish faith?

As I pointed out in the first section of this chapter, the goal of the Law is peace. However, true peace is achieved by practicing the following: 1) "Love the Lord your God with all your heart, and with all your soul, and with all your mind" (Matthew 22:37); and, 2) "Love your neighbor as yourself" (Matthew 22:39). To quote a former "group home" client of mine: *That's it! That's it! And that's all!* In the following section, I will present further evidence that the letter of the Law brings death, but it is the Spirit, rather, that gives life.

CURSED IS EVERYONE WHO HANGS ON A TREE

Further indictment of the sacrificial aspects of the Law of Torah can be found in Paul's letter to the Galatians. In Galatians 3:10–11, Paul contends that everyone who lives under the law is "cursed." His reasoning is that no one can "abide in all things written in the book of the law"; thus, anyone who fails in attempting to do so (*which is everyone*) is cursed. In verse 13, Paul includes Jesus in this curse when he writes: "Christ redeemed us from the curse of the Law, having become a curse for us—for it is written, 'cursed is everyone who hangs on a tree.'"

Here, Paul is referencing Deuteronomy 21:23, but seems to be reinterpreting where the responsibility for the curse lies. Notice the following:

Gal. 3:13: *"For it is written, 'cursed is everyone who hangs on a tree.'"*	Deut. 21:23: *"For anyone hung on a tree is under God's curse."* (NRSV)

Similar to Jesus in Luke 4:18–19 and 7:19–23, where Scripture that includes God's vengeance is eliminated, here Paul is eliminating the idea that it is

God who curses those hung on a tree. What Paul is writing fits perfectly with Jesus, who instructs: "He causes his sun to rise on the evil and the good, and sends rain on the righteous and the unrighteous" (Matthew 5:45). The Law was the ancients' attempt at bringing about peace and order. It was also a death-dealer for Paul and a curse for Jesus.

Paul, earlier in his letter, explains how he began to live for God, however. He writes:

> For through the Law I died to the Law, so that I might live to God. I have been crucified with Christ; and it is no longer I who live, but Christ lives in me; and the life which I now live in the flesh I give by faith in the Son of God, who loved me and gave himself up for me. I do not nullify the grace of God, for if righteousness comes through the Law, then Christ died needlessly. (Gal. 2: 19–21)

Being the good Pharisee he had once been, Paul understood the Law better than anyone. After his dramatic conversion,[23] he finally saw the Law for what it was: a death-dealing curse that killed the very messiah sent to free us. To break free from such a curse, he had to completely die to the Law in order to live for God (2:19). If we follow-suit, we can join as "Abraham's descendants, heirs according to the promise" (3:29).

KILL THE GENTILES

In this section, I would like to provide one final instance where violence in the Old Testament is subverted in the New. Paul, in Romans 15:8–9, quotes from Psalm 18: "For I say that Christ has become a servant to the circumcision on behalf of the truth of God to confirm the promise given to the fathers, and for the Gentiles to glorify God for his mercy; as it is written, 'therefore I will give praise to You among the Gentiles, and I will sing to your name.'" In the psalm from which Paul is quoting, prior to "giving thanks among the nations," (Psalm 18:49) the Psalmist writes of the Gentiles crying out for help but receiving none (18:41) and that God will "execute vengeance" (18:48) and "subdue peoples" (18:48). However, when Paul quotes from this psalm, he completely omits the violent passages.

The exegesis that Paul uses is strikingly similar to that of Jesus. In the first section of this chapter, I discussed how Jesus, in Luke 4:18–19, omits the phrase "and the day of vengeance of our God" from Isaiah 61:1–2. In

---

23. Found in Acts 9: 1–20.

Romans 15, Paul omits the phrase "the God who executes vengeance for me" (Psalm 18:47). As I see it, Paul and Jesus are modeling how Scripture should be read in light of the revelation of God's inclusive and peaceful nature. Their hermeneutics appear consistent with each other—both creative, both sacrifice-subverting.

CONCLUDING REMARKS

Over the past three chapters, I argued that the Bible has a clear trajectory away from sacred violence; citing multiple instances where this can be witnessed. For too long, God, within the Jewish, Christian, and Muslim religious mainstreams, has been viewed as a deity who takes sides and exacts vengeance on the enemies of each faith. However, what *should* set the Christian faith apart is the gospel revelation of Jesus Christ. When Scripture can be viewed through this revelation, rather than the reverse, Christianity can distance herself from the sacrificial religious mindset that has been in place since the dawn of humanity. Michael Hardin sums this up wonderfully in the following: "The violent gods, the gods who need sacrifice, who need victims, who need scapegoats, the gods who demand blood and war and terror and who justify their anger and wrath on the anvil of justice and the rule of law do not exist, except in our imaginations, tyrants made in our own image."[24] These tyrants are not the infinitely good God of the Bible, nor are they the Abba Jesus spoke about. Scripture's internal hermeneutic—the trajectory away from divine violence—gives us this truth and testifies about God's Word, which has always been Christ Jesus.

Before moving on to the Apostle Paul's apparent universalism in the next chapter, I want to leave you with one brief, yet profound thought from *A Relational God of Peace* by Jordan Blevins. He writes: "It [the biblical narrative] is a story of the power of peace, non-violence, and relationship over and through scapegoating and violence. It is a story of a new life—and a story our world needs to hear."[25] I agree with Blevins that the peace of God needs to get out into the world. For too long, Christianity has professed a belief in a violent god, a god that looks little, often nothing, like Jesus. I believe our world is ready to finally hear about the God who behaves exactly like Jesus, who loves exactly like Jesus, and who *is* exactly like Jesus.

24. Hardin, "The God of Pat Robertson," 2.
25. Blevins, "A Relational God of Peace," 23.

PART III

NEW TESTAMENT THEOLOGY

7

Paul: Teacher of Universal Reconciliation?

He is the image of the invisible God, the firstborn of all creation;
For in him all things in heaven and on earth were created, things
visible and invisible,
Whether thrones or dominions or rulers or powers—
All things have been created through him and for him.
He himself is before all things, and in him all things hold together.
He is the head of the body, the church;
He is the beginning, the firstborn from the dead,
So that he might come to have first place in everything.
For in him all the fullness of God was pleased to dwell,
And through him God was pleased to reconcile to himself all things,
Whether on earth or in heaven,
By making peace through the blood of the cross.

Colossians 1:15–20—NRSV

A GREAT MAJORITY OF Scripture in support of universal reconciliation is found in the New Testament; primarily in the writings of Paul. At face value, there appear to be multiple instances in which Paul strongly suggests that all will be reconciled to God in the end. I will discuss a few of these passages at length in the following sections of this chapter.

Although Paul uses the word "all" on multiple occasions in many of his epistles,[1] some assert that throughout the entirety of the New Testament, it is obvious that the word "all" does not in fact mean "all."[2] Some may point to such texts as Romans 14:2, where Paul writes: "One person has faith that he may eat *all* [emphasis mine], but he who is weak eats vegetables only" as proof of such a claim. In this verse, Paul is writing about being non-judgmental over which foods various people eat. Certainly, Paul is not advocating cannibalism or the eating of non-food items; thus, we conclude that he certainly did not literally mean one may eat "all" things. However, there are also instances where Paul's use of the word "all" *is* clearly accepted by mainstream Christianity to be in fact "all." Take, for instance, Ephesians 1:11, in which Paul writes: "according to his purpose who works *all things* [emphasis mine] after the council of his will." Then there is Romans 3:23, which states: "for *all* [emphasis mine] have sinned and fall short of the glory of God."[3] Thus, within Pauline writings, his use of "all" does have ambiguity.

The first two verses I am going to explore in depth are Romans 5:18—19 and 1 Corinthians 15:22. In doing so, I hope to establish just how dissimilar the contexts are between these two passages and that of Romans 14:2. Hence, "all" not meaning "all" in Romans 14:2 (or other verses with related contexts)[4] is hardly an argument that it therefore does not mean "all" in the passages I'm using for the argument at hand. Before I do that, however, I would like to focus my attention on the parallels Paul draws between Adam and Christ (the second Adam), as they both play pivotal roles within the larger contexts in Romans 5:18–19 and 1 Corinthians 15:22.

---

1. For sake of the arguments presented in this book, I will include Romans, 1 and 2 Corinthians, Galatians, Philippians, 1 and 2 Thessalonians, Philemon, Colossians, and Ephesians (although disputed by some scholars) as authored by Paul.

2. For example, Thomas Talbott mentions theologian Loraine Boettner—who claims there are over fifty instances in the New Testament where "all" does not mean "all"—in Talbott, *Inescapable Love of God*, 52.

3. See, also, Romans 8:28 and 1 Corinthians 15:27 for other instances of Paul's use of the word "all."

4. See the fifty instances throughout non-Pauline Scripture, including Luke 21:17; as well as Pauline texts such as Romans 8:32; 16:19. Thomas Talbott explains in further detail in *The Inescapable Love of God*, 51–60.

ADAM AND CHRIST

Michael Hardin, drawing from theologian Ralph Martin, points out the striking similarities between the Genesis narrative of Adam (taken from the Greek Septuagint) and Paul's description of Christ in a portion of an early Christian hymn from Philippians (taken from the Greek New Testament).

| Adam, taken from Genesis 1–3. "Made in divine image, thought it a prize to be grasped at to be as God; and aspired to a reputation. And spurned being God's servant seeking to be in the likeness of God; and being found in fashion as a man (of dust, now doomed). He exalted himself and became disobedient unto death. He was condemned and disgraced."[A] | Jesus Christ, taken from Phil. 2:5–11. "Being the image of God thought it not a prize to be grasped at to be as God; and made himself of no reputation. And took upon himself the form of a servant and was made in the likeness of humanity and being found in fashion as a human. He humbled himself and became obedient unto death. God highly exalted him and gave him the name and rank of Lord."[B] |

A. Hardin, *Jesus Driven Life*, 240–41.
B. Ibid.

The parallelism between Adam and Jesus is such that I cannot for the life of me understand how Western Christians can believe that Adam's "trespass" plays a larger role in the overall scheme of things than Christ's "act of righteousness." Surely, if eternal conscious torment is a reality, then Adam has a greater direct impact on vastly more human souls than Christ. *Is this really what Paul is suggesting?* If not, then it behooves us to look at Romans 5:18–19 and 1 Corinthians 15:22 a little closer and avoid reading into the text the presupposed Western notion of hell.

PAUL'S USE OF "ALL"

Romans 5:18–19 & 1 Corinthians 15:22

"Therefore just as one man's trespass led to condemnation for all, so one man's act of righteousness leads to justification and life for all. For just as by the one man's disobedience the many were made sinners, so by the one man's obedience the many will be made righteous."[5]

ROMANS 5:18–19 NRSV

5. The word "justification" comes from the Greek word *dikaiósis*, which can be translated to "acquittal, justification, a process of absolution."

"For as in Adam all die, so also in Christ all will be made alive."

1 Corinthians 15:22

Because we cannot make sense of any Scripture without the appropriate context, I want to mention the verses that precede Romans 5:18–19. In verse 12, Paul teaches that "through one man sin entered into the world, and death through sin, and so death spread to all men, because all sinned." We can conclude that, in the context of these two passages, any reference to *sinners* would include *all* sinners; and hence, *all* humans (save one).[6]

Paul continues in Romans 5:15: "For if by the transgression of the one the *many* died, much more did the grace of God and the gift by the grace of the one Man, Jesus Christ, abound to the *many*" (emphasis mine). We already learned in verse 12 that "death spread to all men"; yet in verse 15 Paul states that "many died."[7] Certainly, Paul is not contradicting himself and thus, we must conclude that the "many" in verse 15 are in fact the same as the "all" in verse 12. Now, what must be noticed is that the very same "many" who experience death, also experience Christ's "gift of grace," which is "much more" than anything sin or death (the last enemy abolished—1 Corinthians 15:26) can accomplish. One should note that when Paul uses a phrase like "much more," he is using a rabbinic hermeneutical method known as kal va-chomer, translating to "light and heavy."[8] In this technique, great emphasis is placed on *how much more* the "heavy" thing is over the "light" thing. In Romans 5:15, the grace that abounds to the many is so much greater than the death *all* experience. It confounds me how so many people miss this. I cannot help but question: *Because nobody would dispute that the "many" that died because of sin is actually "all," what evidence is there for the fact that the "grace" that abounds to the "many" is not in fact all?* I would argue that, because of the parallelism Paul draws between Adam and Christ (Ephesians 2:5–11), and because of the entire context of Romans 5, I see no reason to conclude anything other than that both "alls"

6. This, of course, does not include Jesus Christ, who did not sin and thus, is not included in the "all" that are associated with Adam.

7. I have heard it argued that, since there are instances in the New Testament where a writer uses the word "many" to describe those who receive salvation (see, for instance, Hebrews 9:28), there must be those who *do not* receive saving grace, or else a stronger word like "all" would have been chosen. Romans 5:12 and 18, when read in context, seem to suggest otherwise.

8. Hardin, *Romans 5:12–21: An Exegesis*, 2.

in verse 18 and both "manys" in verse 19 in fact refer to "all" humans. So, although all are condemned because of Adam's sin, all are justified to life because of Christ's life, death, and resurrection. Thus, once all are made alive, each in his own order (1 Corinthians 15:23), and subjected to the Son (15:24–27), and after *even* Jesus subjects himself to the Father (15:28), God will be "all in all" (15:28). Michael Hardin writes: "Just as Adam's story is the story of everyone, so also the story of Jesus is the story of all. This is why when the early church talked about salvation they referred to Jesus as Lord of all, not just a few, not just some, but all."[9]

There does, however, remain one last verse which some who hold to the Augustinian doctrine of hell contend in fact changes the thrust of the word "all" in Romans 5:18, namely verse 17. Paul writes that "those who receive the abundance of grace and of the gift of righteousness will reign in life through the One, Jesus Christ." Those who use this verse to suggest a modification to the "all" in verse 18 point to the word "receive," and argue that God's grace hinges on our *active* receiving of such grace. The Greek verb translated to "receive" in verse 17 is *lambanō*,[10] which can indeed imply an active "receiving"; but, as philosopher Thomas Talbott notes: "With respect to those contexts, in which the thing received is divine judgment, divine grace, or a divine gift of some kind, Paul may never have used this term in anything but a passive sense."[11]

To see how Paul uses the word *lambanō* in other passages—specifically with regards to receiving something divine—we can look to Romans 1:5, which includes the phrase "through whom we have received grace" and Romans 5:11, which includes "through whom we have now received reconciliation." In both instances, any receiving that occurs seems to be of God's making, rather than of our own. Why would anyone suggest *lambanō* all of a sudden mean something different come verse 17?

Colossians 1:20

"And through him God was pleased to reconcile to himself all things."

---

9. Hardin, *Jesus Driven Life*, 221.

10. Talbott, *Inescapable Love of God*, 58.

11. Ibid.

In this portion of what is yet another early Christian hymn, found in Paul's letter to the Colossians, Paul again seems to suggest that "all" will be reconciled to God in the end when he writes: "through him God was pleased to reconcile to himself all things." Amongst these "all things" are the "visible and invisible (. . .) thrones, dominions, rulers, and powers" (1:16) that are also known throughout Scripture as the "kingdoms of men."[12] In fact, these kingdoms seem at "the devil's" disposal, when they are offered to Jesus in Matthew 4:8–11. So how, specifically, does Jesus reconcile these principalities, including those ruled by "the satanic," that continually pit themselves against God?

In chapter 5, I discussed how the death and resurrection of Jesus completely turned on its head the way in which humans do culture and religion; which is always through sacred violence. The Romans used the cross to spill blood in order to bring about *Pax Romana*, or Roman Peace. Jesus, however, reconciles all things, including the very "rulers and powers" that broke his body "by making peace through the blood of his cross" (1:20). In doing so, the *Logos* of God (as he is described in John's gospel), who had all things come "into being through him" (John 1:3), will "come to have first place in everything" (Colossians 1:18). It is through peace that Jesus rules like a lion (Revelation 5:5); but when actually revealed, is like a lamb (Revelation 5:6).

Where in Romans 5:18 and 1 Corinthians 15:22 Paul uses the parallelism of Adam and Christ to argue for the saving of all sinners, he expands that concept to "all things," including those powers and principalities that stand in direct opposition to the kingdom of God.

Romans 11:32

"For God has shut up all in disobedience so that he may show mercy to all."

As I mentioned in chapter 1, justice is an important theme in this book. Unfortunately, many Christians conclude that justice is synonymous with wrath—likely due to God's justice being presupposed as retributive. Paul, in Romans 11, offers some insight into how mercy and wrath are not in competition with each other, but do, in fact, complement one another.

Some Christians (primarily Calvinists) often use Romans 9:22–23 to argue for their idea of "election." They read: "What if God, although willing

---

12. See Revelation 11:15.

to demonstrate his wrath and to make his power known, endured with much patience vessels of wrath prepared for destruction? And he did so to make known the riches of his glory upon vessels of mercy, which he prepared beforehand for glory . . . " A *prima facie* reading seems to lead one to conclude a dualistic ending to the human drama—that some are indeed "objects of God's wrath" while others are "objects of his mercy." However, as Michael Hardin once pointed out to me, "text without context is a pre-text." Thus, because the complete context of Romans 9 includes chapters 10 and 11, we must read on.

In Romans 11:22, Paul seems to imply that those who fall experience God's mercy/wrath as "severity," but that those who "continue in his kindness" experience it as "kindness." If you are cut off (11:22), Paul argues that you can again be "grafted in again" (11:23)—for "all Israel will be saved" (11:26). Then he culminates what he began back in Romans 9:1 with: "For just as you once were disobedient to God, but now have been shown mercy because of their disobedience, so these also now have been disobedient, that because of the mercy shown to you they also may now be shown mercy. For God has shut up all in disobedience so that he may show mercy to all." (Rom. 11:30–32) The "disobedient" are the very same "vessels of wrath" from Romans 9:22—the lost, damned, unbelieving Jews (Rom. 9:3–4)—the "non-elect." Yet Paul says they "also may now be shown mercy." No wonder Paul states that God's justice is "unsearchable" (Romans 11:33). Certainly, any justice that is compatible with mercy for *all* cannot be accepted by the majority of men, who demand justice to be retributive.

For Calvinists to "proof-text" Romans 9:22 in favor of their doctrine of "election" is rather unfortunate. I cannot reconcile Paul stating, "so that he that may show mercy to all" with the fact that *traditional doctrine* accepts the eternal torture of billions of humans. It seems either Paul was really confusing—borderline bi-polar—or, he believed God will have mercy on all. In light of his entire argument (Romans 9–11), I cannot think of a serious third option.

YEAH, BUT, PAUL ALSO TAUGHT. . .

Some may be inclined to "push back" against Paul's apparent "Universalism"—and I do not necessarily blame them. Certainly, Paul wrote about potentially suffering "*eternal destruction*" (*olethron aiōnion*) and "*destruction of the flesh*" in his letters to various churches.[13] In the following chapter, I will address 2 Thessalonians 1:8–9, which in most English Bibles seems to suggest that Paul argues some will "be punished with everlasting destruction and shut out from the presence of the Lord and from the glory of his might" (NIV). To address this phrase, I will also discuss the Pauline idea of "destruction of the flesh," which is dissimilar to the Gnostic view that some, such as Philip J. Lee, have noticed has been embraced by American Protestantism as a whole.[14]

Because of the ambiguity of language, we should not simply presuppose *common English interpretations* of such words as "destruction" and "flesh." Furthermore, because a "plain reading" of Scripture will never suffice as a proper hermeneutic, we must define our terms the same way Second Temple Jews did because, like I mentioned before, that is precisely the context of the New Testament.[15]

> *If we have not carefully thought about these things, then prudence must be taken before flippantly blurting: yeah, but, Paul also taught. . .*

---

13. See 2 Thessalonians 1:8—9 and 1 Corinthians 5:5, respectfully.

14. In Gnosticism, the "flesh" is viewed as 100 percent "bad." Most Gnostics shunned the "material world," and instead, embraced the "spiritual world." In short, they were dualists. For a detailed look at the relationship between Gnosticism and Protestantism, see *Against the Protestant Gnostics* by Philip J. Lee.

15. Regarding Paul in a broader sense, one could write thousands and thousands of contradictory books, essays, articles, poems, songs . . . *anything!* With that in mind, I realize that my eschatological conclusions, which are in-part based on Paul's writings, could be misinterpretations of what is supposed to be the "true meaning." I have carefully considered this; which is why I place such emphasis in studying pre and post-conversion Paul; studying how the Pharisees interpreted Hebrew scriptures (as Paul was at one point one); studying a Greek rhetorical technique known as *prosopopoeia*, a technique Paul often used in his own writing; studying anything one can in order to better discern these complicated matters.

8

The Purpose of "Punishment"

I am the way into the city of woe,
I am the way into eternal pain,
I am the way to go among the lost.

Justice caused my high architect to move,
Divine omnipotence created me,
The highest wisdom, and the primal love.

Before me there were no created things
But those that last forever—as do I.
Abandon all hope you who enter here.

—Dante Alighieri[1]

IF YOU OPEN UP your English Bible, you will see the word "hell" mentioned anywhere from thirteen times in the New International Version to fifty-four instances in the King James Version. On top of that, there are presuppositions believers and non-believers alike learn and understand about the Western Christian version of hell prior to understanding how to think or reason. First, it is assumed that the traditional understanding of hell is that it is a place of tremendous torment, both physically and psychologically. Second, this torment lasts for all of eternity, with no hope for reprieve even for a moment. As I have personally discovered, to question this traditional

1. Dante, *Inferno*, Canto III, Lines 1–9.

89

understanding is to "question everything Christianity stands for"—at least according to a few Christians I have come across.

This mindset most likely arises due to pastors and theologians who assert Jesus taught about "hell" more than any other doctrine. What is worse, they then claim he taught that "hell" and "eternal conscious torment" are synonymous and that Christ, along with the Apostles, make this "clear" in scripture. The problem is that there is no evading the fact that, in this view, God, who is "Love,"[2] sends people who do not choose his son in this life to everlasting torment. Those who contend that the wicked choose their eternal destiny still cannot escape the fact that, in their theology, everlasting torment exists in the first place. This can only beg the question as to why God, who is also "Light"[3] and in whom there is no darkness, created, or in the future will create, a place of utter darkness.

So, if our traditional idea of hell is not in fact traditional, as discussed in chapter 2—if the Augustinian understanding of the afterlife is incorrect—what *is* going on with all this "hell" talk in the New Testament?

A VALLEY, A LAKE, AND PLENTY OF FIRE AND BRIMSTONE

Located just south of Jerusalem lies the Valley of the Son of Hinnom, from which the name "Gehenna" is derived. Gehenna occurs twelve times in the New Testament and in all but one instance (James 3:6) was uttered by Jesus.[4] In most English Bibles, the term "hell" is translated predominantly from the word "Gehenna." Historically speaking, this was a place of abomination, considered cursed by the Hebrew people due to their sacrificing of children to various Baalim and Canaanite gods, including Molech. Jeremiah 19:2–6 reads:

2. See 1 John 4:8.

3. See 1 John 1:5.

4. To the Gentiles, those with whom Paul was commissioned to share the Gospel, "Gehenna" is never mentioned; yet in the book of Acts, it is written that Paul "did not shrink from declaring to you the *whole* [emphasis mine] purpose of God" (Acts 26:27). How can one reconcile the fact that Paul never wrote about Gehenna, while contending that he did not shrink from declaring the "whole purpose of God"? Certainly, he could have used a similar analogy that the Gentiles would be familiar with, yet he did not. Paul did talk about death, destruction, and punishment, but like I keep mentioning, "we must define our terms." Later in this chapter, I will discuss the Pauline understanding of these words.

Then go out to the valley of Ben-hinnom, which is by the entrance of the potsherd gate, and proclaim there the words that I tell you, and say, "hear the word of the Lord, O kings of Judah and inhabitants of Jerusalem: thus says the Lord of hosts, the God of Israel, 'Behold I am about to bring a calamity upon this place, at which the ears of everyone that hears of it will tingle. Because they have forsaken me and have made this an alien place and have burned sacrifices in it to other gods, that neither they nor their forefathers nor the kings of Judah had ever known, and because they have filled this place with the blood of the innocent and have built the high places of Baal to burn their sons in the fire as burnt offerings to Baal, a thing which I never commanded or spoke of, nor did it ever enter my mind; therefore, behold, days are coming,' declares the Lord, 'when this place will no longer be called Topheth or the valley of Ben-hinnom, but rather the valley of Slaughter.'[5]

Later, the valley would become Jerusalem's place of refuse, where trash and filth, as well as the bodies of criminals, were discarded and burned so as to not allow them to rot and decay. From the fires within the valley, smoke would be seen rising above the crests and became known by *some* to symbolize the future punishment of the wicked. To the Jewish people, this was a place of calamity and sorrow, where the "worm dies not" (Mark 9:48). Moreover, in a prophetic sense, it was a place Jesus warned his followers about.[6] As we know, most did not take heed.

In 70 CE, when the Roman army sacked Jerusalem, they left no building standing, including the Temple. Those who did not heed Christ's warnings about their violence and subsequent coming destruction were killed and disposed of in the Valley of the Son of Hinnom and nearby rivers (so many of them that they would be carried into a nearby lake). It was essentially the end of the world as far as the Jews were concerned. First-century historian Josephus writes:

Now, this destruction that fell upon the Jews, as it was not inferior to any of the rest in itself, so did it still appear greater than it really was; and this, because not only the whole of the country through which they had fled was filled with *slaughter* [emphasis mine], and Jordan could not be passed over, by reason of the dead bodies that

---

5. See also 2 Chronicles 33:6, Jeremiah 7:31, and 2 Kings 23:10.
6. See Matthew 24.

were in it, but because the Lake Asphaltites (Dead Sea) was also full of dead bodies, that were carried down into it by the river.[7]

In the following paragraph, I will discuss how Jesus' warnings about Gehenna should be applied to our lives today. However, Gehenna should not *only* be viewed as a potential eschatological punishment for the wicked. It was, in fact, a very real warning to those to whom Jesus was preaching, one that, as I mentioned before, came to pass in the first century. In fact, on numerous occasions, such as in Matthew 24:34, Jesus tells his disciples that "this generation will not pass away" until the things prophesized in Matthew 24 come to pass. These things included the destruction of the temple (24:1–2), the signs of the end of the age (24:3–8), the desolating sacrilege (24:15–28), and the coming of the Son of Man (24:29–31).

So what then, if not merely a two-thousand year old warning about the destruction of Jerusalem at the hands of the Romans, does Jesus have to say about "Gehenna" that we can apply to our lives today? Without reading into Scripture the Western idea of hell, let's look in the Gospel of Mark, in which Jesus uses "Gehenna" in the following manner:

> And if thy hand may cause thee to stumble, cut it off; it is better for thee maimed to enter into the life, than having the two hands, to go away to the gehenna, to the fire—the unquenchable—where their worm is not dying, and the fire is not being quenched. And if thy foot cause thee to stumble, cut it off; it is better for thee to enter into the life lame, than having the two feet to be cast to the gehenna, to the fire—the unquenchable—where their worm is not dying, and the fire is not being quenched. And if thine eye may cause thee to stumble, cast it out; it is better for thee one-eyed to enter the reign of God, than having two eyes, to be cast to the gehenna of the fire—where their worm is not dying, and the fire is not being quenched; for every one with fire shall be salted, and every sacrifice with salt shall be salted. The salt [is] good, but if the salt may become saltless, in what will ye season [it]? Have in yourselves salt, and have peace in one another. (Mark 9:43–50 YLT)[8]

This certainly is a stern warning; one that should get our attention. I do not believe this passage is teaching eternal torment, however. Bradley Jersak has this to say about interpreting Gehenna as eternal torment:

---

7. Flavius, *Wars of the Jews*, Book IV, Chapter VII, Section 6.

8. See also, Matthew 5:29–30; 18:8–9.

We ought to also note the irony and incongruence of the Church utilizing the very place where God became violently offended by the literal burning of children as our primary metaphor for a final and eternal burning of God's wayward people in literal flames. Thus, God becomes the very Molech who decrees that the angels must deliver his children to the flames, even though this was the very reason he ordered Hinnom to be deserted in the first place![9]

So, if Jersak is correct in his assessment (and I believe he is), can the flames of Gehenna be restorative rather than literal torture devices for those who fail to "get in"?

First, notice how Jesus states "for everyone with fire shall be salted" (9:49); thus, in one manner or another, all will have to suffer trials and tribulations—all will be judged. This is described as a "good" thing in verse 50, but is also described as "unquenchable" in verses 43 and 48. What is "unquenchable fire" if not "eternal torment"? Paul, in 1 Corinthians 3:12–15, gives us insight when he writes:

> Now if any man builds on the foundation with gold, silver, precious stones, wood, hay, straw, each man's work will become evident; for the day will show it because it is to be revealed with fire, and the fire itself will test the quality of each man's work. If any man's work which he has built on it remains, he will receive a reward. If any man's work is burned up, he will suffer loss; but he himself will be saved, yet so as through fire.

Once something is burnt up—when all the "stuff" (wood, hay, and straw) is burnt away—the fire does not continue to burn and torment that which was once burnt.[10]

So, assuming Jesus is not literally advocating self-mutilation, what *is* burned up in the "unquenchable fire" he speaks of? Why are the hand, foot, and eye cast into the fire in order for the person to experience life? I believe it is specifically because it is these that cause us to sin the most. The hands, feet, and eyes are the causal sources of that which creates mere "wood, hay, and straw" in our lives. In other words, the "flesh" must be destroyed.

---

9. Jersak, *Her Gates*, 65.

10. My stepfather is a retired firefighter. Growing up, I became well aware of the three elements of fire: heat, oxygen, and fuel. Once a fire ran out of any of these three key elements, the fire would go out. Without any fuel, there is nothing to burn up any longer.

While this devotion to live like Christ can be trying, it is the *one thing* that "seasons" and "preserves" our lives with salt.[11] However, if we fail or refuse to recognize this, we will become "tasteless" and "no longer good for anything"—in danger of being thrown into Gehenna. Thus, in one way or another, our former sinful nature must be burned away; either by living in relationship with Christ in the present or accepting a two-fold fate—sin that leads to self-destructive consequences and *God's purifying punishment in the future.* I love how Jersak flips the "traditional" Western idea of hell on its head, concluding that even Gehenna is "good news." He writes:

> While the legacy of Gehenna stands as a genuine warning of destruction to those who persist in rebellion and idolatry, Jeremiah and Jesus forewarn us to avoid the consequential wrath. For those who experience the calamities of the "way of death," the invitation is extended to a New Covenant of restoration. Sin and its consequences are overcome by redemption and restoration (. . .) the church can hold out the New Covenant of Jesus in which even the Valley of Slaughter is sanctified, every curse of destruction is broken, and God's exiles find their way home.[12]

A Burning Lake of Fire

The Book of Revelation has some of the starkest imagery in the entire Bible. Some of the most intense and brutal depictions are when all those who come to make war against Christ, including the Beast and the kings of the immoral nations of the earth (19:19),[13] are cast alive into the "lake of fire" (19:20). However, are passages like this meant to be interpreted as a hopeless ending for some? Before I answer that, I would like to offer an Old Testament example of something being destroyed by fire, namely, the city of Sodom. Let's take a look at Ezekiel 16:53–55. After all of the fire and brimstone, we learn that:

> Nevertheless, I will restore their captivity, the captivity of Sodom and her daughters, the captivity of Samaria and her daughters, and along with them your own captivity, in order that you may bear your humiliation and feel ashamed for all that you have done when you become a consolation to them. Your sisters, Sodom with

11. Think, in terms of "preserving" and "seasoning" meat, for instance.

12. Jersak, *Her Gates*, 65.

13. See Revelation 11:2, 9, 19; 14:8; 17:2, 10–12, 15, 18. Ibid., 166.

her daughters and Samaria with her daughters, will return to their
former state, and you with your daughters will also return to your
former state.

Where once there was utter destruction for Sodom, the promise is that
she will be restored. Thus, even a "lake of fire and brimstone" (Revelation
20:10) need *not* be seen as hopeless.

In Revelation 21, we learn who is specifically cast into the lake of fire.
Verse 8 tells us: "for the cowardly and unbelieving and abominable and
murderers and immoral persons and sorcerers and idolaters and all liars,
their part will be in the lake that burns with fire and brimstone, which is the
second death."[14] They are described as dogs, sorcerers, immoral persons,
murderers, idolaters, and liars—being rightly located outside the gates of
New Jerusalem (Revelation 22:15). Yet, the writer leaves open a hopeful
vision that all will be permitted to enter the city, so long as their "robes are
washed in the blood of the Lamb" (22:14).

Notice in Revelation 21:24 that "the nations will walk by its light,
and the kings of the earth will bring their glory into it." These should be
seen as none other than the "kings of the earth" who, along with the Beast,
were cast into the lake of fire in Revelation 19:19. They are the leaders of
nations who stand in opposition to God. They are the warmongers—the
death-dealers—Babylon. Yet, they enter the city. *How?* The writer goes on
to envision the gates of New Jerusalem never closing (21:25) with a "tree of
life," whose leaves will be "for the healing of the nations" (22:2). They cannot enter the city until their robes are washed clean, as "nothing unclean,
and no one who practices abomination and lying, shall ever come into it,
but only those whose names are written in the Lamb's book of life" (21:27).
However, this warning should not be seen as hopeless, as the Spirit and
the bride (followers of Christ) will be calling to those who thirst (22.17)
because the invitation from Jesus will remain open (21:6).

Although the imagery of a lake of fire and brimstone should be taken
quite seriously, it should not be used to argue in favor of a hopeless, literal
torture chamber that awaits the wicked. Rather, there seems to be a hopeful
ending, where Jesus Christ keeps his invitation to drink from the water of
life open, where the Spirit and the bride of Christ call others to "come,"
and where the gates of New Jerusalem remain open for those in the lake of
fire—those outside the city—to finally come home.

---

14. As I will discuss in the third section of this chapter, we must die to our former
self in order to live for Christ. Thus, all will go through two deaths eventually.

THE POWER TO DESTROY

"Do not fear those who kill the body but are unable to kill the soul; but rather fear Him who is able to destroy both soul and body in hell (Gehenna)." Matthew 10:28[15]

Some will argue that this phrase in the book of Matthew points to compelling proof that God *can* and *will* allow the eternal torment of some (sinners). However, it is my belief that to interpret this passage as such is to lift it from the immediate context of what is being taught. Earlier, Jesus warns his followers in verse 16 that they will be sent out "as sheep in the midst of wolves," leading to hatred toward them and ultimately, death (10:21–22). However, he follows this by giving comfort to his disciples by declaring: "do not fear them (10:28)," for the Father does not even allow a "two-cent sparrow to (. . .) fall to the ground (10:29)," because we are "of more value than many sparrows" (10:30). Now, that being said let us get into the more troubling passage—namely verse 28.

As I discussed in the previous section, "everyone will be salted with fire," which is "good"; thus, even the fires of Gehenna are for "seasoning" and "preserving" (Mark 9:49). With that in mind, coupled with the comfort Jesus had just offered his disciples, how should this passage be interpreted, hopeful or hopeless? Jesus here seems to be suggesting that his disciples should not live in fear that God *could* destroy them in how we may think of the word now, but rather, that his Father values even a lowly sparrow enough to not let them "fall to the ground," so, imagine how much greater his love for humanity, which is made in his "image and likeness." Surely, he has the power to destroy, but as a God who even loves the birds of the air, how should "destroy" be interpreted?

It is important to note the Greek verb translated to "destroy" is *apollumi*, and is the same word used in the Parable of the Lost Sheep and the Parable of the Prodigal Son. In both cases, that which was once lost, or perished (*apollumi*), is now found. Take a look, also, at 1 Peter 1:7, which reads: "So that the proof of your faith, being more precious than gold which is *perishable* [emphasis mine], even though tested by fire, may be found to result in praise and glory and honor at the revelation of Jesus Christ." The testing of gold by fire is the process of refining—the destruction of impurities in the metal. Any person destroyed by God in the fires of Gehenna

15. See also Luke 12:5.

would be destroyed in the same manner gold is destroyed in a fire. The purpose, of course, is for refinement.

ETERNAL PUNISHMENT, DESTRUCTION & SEPARATION

In addition to Jesus' use of the word "Gehenna," there are many other passages that adherents of eternal torment point to in an attempt to further argue that the Bible teaches such a doctrine. While some of the parables Jesus used are harsh, they should not be used to instill paralyzing fear. In fact, "if perfect love casts out fear" (1 John 4:18), the passages that follow should be handled with great care so as not to flippantly conclude something that may not be there. All too often, the parables that Jesus used to challenge the beliefs of his followers are forced into rigid, systematic ways of thinking. What people need to understand, though, is that parables are pedagogical, and not meant to be interpreted literally. Thus, using a literalist hermeneutic for interpreting a parable that cannot be interpreted literally seems rather illogical.

The Sheep and the (Baby) Goats

Matthew 25:31–46 seems to be the first place many Christians go to "clearly" point out that some sinners will be lost forever. Some contend that Jesus is simply giving his listeners a rather detailed explanation as to how he will divide up all people: some to "eternal punishment" (*aiōnios kólasis*) and some to "eternal life" (*aiōnios zōē*). However, I believe that while that is certainly taking place, much more is going on.

In verse 32, Jesus gathers "all the nations . . . as the shepherd separates the sheep *(próbaton)* from the goats *(ériphos)*."[16] When Jesus gathers "all the nations," it appears as if he views *all* [humans] as a part of the flock. Moreover, his use of *ériphos*, which literally means "baby goats," seems to be intentional. One could discern that, since Jesus contrasts "punishment" (*kolasis*) with "life" (*zōē*), He is also contrasting "baby goats" (*ériphos*), with "mature sheep" (*próbaton)—all* a part of the flock. This context will be pivotal in how we exegete the rest of the parable.

---

16. The word translated "sheep" is *próbaton* and refers to *any animal that grazes* (goes out to pasture), but especially to *sheep*. Furthermore, *ériphos* specifically refers to "baby, or kid goats."

After Christ places the sheep on his right and the goats on the left, he begins to explain what characterizes a mature sheep. Jesus says in verses 35–36: "For I was hungry, and you gave me something to eat; I was thirsty, and you gave me something to drink; I was a stranger, and you invited me in; naked, and you clothed me; I was sick, and you visited me; I was in prison, and you came to me." Because of this, those on his right "inherit the kingdom prepared for you from the foundation of the world (25:34)." What is interesting is that the sheep then question when they did these things and Christ responds "truly I say to you, to the extent that you did it to one of these brothers of mine, *even* the least *of them*, you did it to me" (25:40). In other words, mature sheep instinctively do the will of Jesus—having possibly never heard the name—when they take care of the least of humanity; namely the poor, suffering, and down-trodden. *They may in fact not be "Christians" at all—let the implications of that set in for a moment.*

In contrast, those on the left are commanded to depart "into the eternal *(aiōnios)* fire which has been prepared for the devil and his angels (25:41)." They are the baby goats of the flock precisely because they gave "the least of these" nothing to eat or drink, no invitation into their homes, no clothing for the naked, and did not visit the condemned in prison. Like the sheep, they too seem surprised by this and I would argue that it is because they believed *themselves* worthy to be called "Christian." However, because they acted not like the mature sheep of the flock, but like baby goats instead, they find themselves condemned—opposite from what they initially seemed to think. If you adhere to eternal torment, *let the implications of that also set in for a moment.*

Jesus concludes the parable by saying: "these (baby goats on the left) will go away into eternal punishment (*aiōnios kólasis*), but the righteous (mature sheep on the right) into eternal life (*aiōnios zōē*)" (25:46). It is precisely this passage which many then proof-text to conclude that some human beings will find themselves separated from God forever—in everlasting punishment. However, one need not be a Greek scholar to understand the phrase *aiōnios kólasis* does not have a "one-size-fits-all" translation of "everlasting punishment." To understand why, I will first discuss the word *aiōnios* and how to properly understand it.

Aiōnios

The word *aiōnios*, strictly speaking, translates as "age-enduring." On one hand, some uses of the word *aiōnios* can seem to imply "eternal" or "everlasting." Take for example, Romans 16:26, where Paul writes: "according to the commandment of the eternal (*aiōnios*) God." In this instance, the translation of *aiōnios* should be "eternal." However, as Thomas Talbott contends: "For however we translate aiōnios, it is clearly an adjective and must therefore function like an adjective; and adjectives often vary in meaning, sometimes greatly, when the nouns they qualify signify different categories of things."[17] You only need to go back one verse to Romans 16:25 to see how *aiōnios* is used to describe something that we all now know *came to an end*. Verse 25 reads: "Now to him who is able to establish you according to my gospel and the preaching of Jesus Christ, according to the revelation of the mystery which has been kept secret for long ages (*chronois aiōnios*) past." Certainly, Paul knew the "age-enduring mystery" ended with the revelation of Jesus Christ, and yet uses *aiōnios* anyway.[18] Hence, *aiōnios* can describe something that is "eternal" or "temporal."

To use an Old Testament example, we can look at Habakkuk 3:6, where both *mountains that have collapsed* and *God* are qualified by *olam* (the Hebrew equivalent of *aiōnios*), in the same verse. Yet, some still argue in the following manner: *If aiōnios does not mean "eternal" in regards to punishment for the wicked, then it also does not mean the life for the righteous is "eternal."* Like I have mentioned on numerous occasions, we must define our terms. *What does eternal mean?* More specifically, as there are obviously multiple interpretations, what does it mean in this context?

I believe we must view the word *aiōnios* in a qualitative sense, rather than a quantitative one. In other words, the word does not imply a minute by minute—*add up all the time*—understanding. Of the word, J.W. Hanson concludes:

> Hence it follows that the readers of the Bible are under the most imperative obligations to understand the word in all cases as denoting limited duration, unless the subject treated, or other qualifying words compel them to understand it differently. There is nothing in the derivation, lexicography, or usage of the word to

---

17. Talbott, *Inescapable Love of God*, 80.
18. Ibid., 79.

warrant us in understanding it to convey the thought of endless duration.[19]

I do not suggest that eternal life with God will be limited in duration, because life with the Father—who is the sustainer of life—qualifies *aiōnios* as such. Regarding *aiōnios zōē*, or eternal life with God, Thomas Talbott puts it this way: "For whereas the life (*zōē*), being rightly related to God, is clearly an end in itself—that is, valuable or worth having for its own sake."[20] One could then ask: why would *kólasis* not qualify *aiōnios* as unending in duration? To answer that, in the following section, I will discuss how the Greek word *kólasis* is to be understood.

Kólasis

> The punishment (*kólasis*) is (. . .) a means to an end. And given the history of the word kólasis, it most likely signifies a means to the end of being rightly related to God.[21]

The Greek philosopher Plato understood the word *kólasis* to not only mean punishment, but the specific type of punishment that is for the ultimate benefit of the one being punished. He writes:

> If you will think, Socrates, of what punishment (*kólasis*) can do for the evildoer, you will see at once that in the opinion of mankind virtue may be acquired. No one punishes the evildoer under the notion, or for the reason that, he has done wrong—only the unreasonable fury of a beast is so vindictive . . . He punishes for the sake of prevention, thereby clearly implying that virtue is capable of being taught. This is the notion of all who punish others either privately or publicly. And Athenians, especially your fellow citizens no less than other men, punish and correct all whom they regard as evildoers. And hence we may infer them to be of the number of those who think that virtue may be acquired and taught.[22]

Greek scholar William Barclay points out the word *kólasis* originally described the cutting off of tree branches to encourage growth.[23] Unlike the

---

19. Hanson, *The Greek Word Aion—Aionios*, "Conclusion."

20. Talbott, *Inescapable Love of God*, 81.

21. Ibid.

22. Plato, *Protagoras*, 324.

23. Barclay, *William Barclay*, 66.

historic meaning of the Greek word *timōría,* which implies a more vengeful punishment, *kólasis* was for the purpose of correction.[24] Thus, a reading of Matthew 25:46 would more specifically read as follows: "these will go away into *age-enduring/eternal correction,* but the righteous into *age-enduring/ eternal life.*" For the sake of argument, even a reading of "eternal correction or corrective punishment" need not be seen as hopeless punishment.[25] Like Talbott, I must agree that the "eternal corrective punishment," like the "eternal life," is an end of sorts. The *life* is the quality (or type) of life one would have if reconciled unto God, while the punishment is a *last means* by which one can possibly be reconciled unto God.[26] The achieved goal of God's punishment, namely "correction," will in fact be "eternal,"

Eternal Destruction & Separation

Where can I go from your Spirit? Or where can I flee from your presence? If I ascend to heaven, you are there; if I make my bed in Sheol, you are there. If I take the wings of the morning and settle at the farthest limits of the sea, even there your hand shall lead me, and your right hand shall hold me fast. Psalm 139: 7–10

Another common passage "traditionalists" use as an argument for eternal torment is 2 Thessalonians 1:9, which reads: "They will be punished with everlasting destruction and shut out from the presence of the Lord and from the glory of his might" (NIV). Similar to Jeremiah 7:22, the translators of the New International Version have manipulated the original language in order to make it fit their doctrinal statements. The literal translation is as follows: "Who shall suffer justice—destruction age-enduring—from the face of the Lord, and from the glory of his strength." (YLT) The first thing I would like to point out is that the NIV translators have rendered "*aiōnios*" as "everlasting." As I discussed at length earlier in this section, *aiōnios* should not be assumed as "unending temporal duration," which the translation to "everlasting" does. For sake of this particular argument, I would be

---

24. *Kólasis* implies "chastisement/punishment" and comes from the root word, *kolazó,* which means "correction." *Timōría,* on the other hand, means "punishment/ penalty" and comes from the root word *timóreó,* which means "punishment/vengeance."

25. As I mention in the previous chapter, Paul certainly did not see the "vessels of wrath" remaining in that state forever—hopelessly cut off, if you will. He envisioned a time when the "vessels of wrath" would be "grafted back in" (Romans 11:23).

26. Talbott, *Inescapable Love of God,* 81.

comfortable with "eternal," given how I believe the word is best understood (see my exegesis of Matthew 25:46).

An unfortunate presupposition many carry into their reading of this text is that "eternal destruction" should be seen as a hopeless ending. Certainly, this *is* a harsh passage. But, let us look at what Paul says about destruction in his letter to the Corinthians, so we can have a clear picture as to how it should be interpreted. He writes: "I have decided to deliver such a one to Satan for the destruction of his flesh, so that his spirit may be saved in the day of the Lord Jesus" (1 Corinthians 5:5). Paul does not seem to think that destruction would lead to the complete material and spiritual death of a person, or at least, it does not appear so in this passage. Moreover, when Paul does talk about death (as in Romans 7:9–10), he does not talk about it in terms of complete annihilation or eternal hopelessness, as he states that death had already occurred in his own life. In fact, this same type of death, or "destruction of the flesh," must occur in order to live for Christ. Romans 6:7–8 states: "For he who has died is freed from sin. Now if we have died with Christ, we believe that we shall also live with him." As Christians, we should recognize the notion that our old self must be put to death in order for Christ to live through us. I believe it is this type of death that must occur in order for us all to pass through the fires of judgement. As I discussed in the first section of this chapter, "everyone will be salted with fire" (Mark 9:49), even those of us who follow Jesus, as "each man's work" will be "revealed with fire" (1 Corinthians 3:13). This fire is specifically the mechanism that allows all the junk, waste, and filth to be burned away, but it should not be seen as something that destroys the spirit, where the person is lost entirely.

So, what specifically, would a New Testament understanding of "the destruction of flesh" be, if not the Gnostic notion of "the entire body"? In his letter to the Galatians Paul writes, of the "flesh,"

> Now the deeds of the flesh are evident, which are: immorality, impurity, sensuality, idolatry, sorcery, enmities, strife, jealousy, outbursts of anger, disputes, dissensions, factions, envying, drunkenness, carousing, and things like these, of which I forewarn you, just as I have forewarned you, that those who practice such things will not inherit the kingdom of God. (Galatians 5: 19–21)[27]

The destruction of the deeds above, or the "flesh," is what must occur in order for the *spirit* to "be saved in the day of the Lord Jesus" (1 Corinthians

27. I will discuss "the kingdom of God" in chapter 9.

5:5). Thomas Talbott summarizes this beautifully in the following: "In a very real sense, then—the Pauline sense, if you will—both Abram and Saul were utterly destroyed and destroyed forever; what they had thought themselves to be, what they had called themselves, no longer existed."[28]

Now, back to 2 Thessalonians 1:9: if aiōnios is not "unending temporal duration," and destruction is not "annihilation," but that which saves the spirit, where does the phrase "shut out from the presence of the Lord" come from?

In order to address this, I would like to focus my attention on the Greek word, apo, translated to "from" in English. At times, the word can imply "shut out," or "away from," and yet at other times, it means simply "from." I will place two passages; side by side; to show you what I mean.

"And they said to the mountains and to the rocks, 'fall on us and hide us *from (apo) the presence of him* who sits on the throne . . . '" Revelation 6:16—emphasis mine	"Therefore repent and return, so that your sins may be wiped away, in order that times of refreshing may come *from (apo) the presence of the Lord . . .*" Acts 3:19—emphasis mine

When comparing 2 Thessalonians 1:9 with both Revelation 6:16 and Acts 3:19, the only dissimilar verse I notice of the three is Revelation 6:16, where the "from" (apo), is modified by the phrase "fall on us and hide us from (apo) the presence of him who sits on the throne."[29] Thus, the most appropriate interpretation of the word "apo" in Revelation 6:16 is "away from." In both 2 Thessalonians 1:9 and Acts 3:19, however, the exact same Greek phrase "apo prosōpou tou Kyriou" is used. Notice the following:

"Eternal destruction from the presence of the Lord" (olethron aionion apo prosōpou tou Kyriou) 2 Thessalonians 1:9	"Times of refreshing from the presence of the Lord" (kairoi anapsyxeos apo prosōpou tou Kyriou) Acts 3:19

There seems no reason both "times of refreshing" and "destruction" should not be thought to come directly from (apo) the presence of the Lord.

There is nothing outside of the less-than-compelling interpretation of 2 Thessalonians 1:8–9 that suggest some will be "eternally separated" from God—and let's not forget the metaphysical absurdity of separation from an omnipresent deity. Rather, upon closer examination of the Greek words used, combined with yet another manipulation by NIV translators,

28. Talbott, *Inescapable Love of God*, 93.
29. Ibid., 89–90.

I believe it does not in fact teach either "eternal separation from God" or "complete spiritual and material destruction of the self."

THE RICH MAN AND LAZARUS

As I mentioned earlier, parables are pedagogical—meant for teaching. Although many argue that the parable of the rich man and Lazarus is "plainly" teaching eternal torment, I will offer my explanation as to why I believe this is incorrect.

First, this parable is not entirely original to Jesus; rather, it draws its origins from an Egyptian folk-tale.[30] In the Egyptian version, Si-Osiris journeys to the underworld and discovers the reversal of fates for both a rich and poor man. The tale concludes with: "he who has been good on earth will be blessed in the kingdom of the dead, and he who has been evil on earth, will suffer in the kingdom of the dead."[31] *Sound familiar?* In the parable of the rich man and Lazarus, found in Luke 16:19–31, a rich man who lives a life of luxury refuses to offer any aid to a poor beggar named Lazarus—who is described as "covered with sores" (16:20). When they die, however, the tables are turned (similar to the parable of the sheep and goats). Lazarus ends up in "Abraham's bosom"; while the rich man cries out for water due to the agony he is in (16:23–24). Between them lies a "great chasm" that "none may cross over" (16:26). In the immediate context, what lends one to conclude some are lost forever? Is not the heart of the gospel the news that the "great chasm" was bridged when Jesus died for our sins?

There is a message here—a teaching that we must pay attention to. When we think ourselves worthy, or in this case rich and haughty, we will find ourselves "least" in the kingdom of heaven (Matthew 5:19)—included, but *least*. Take a look at the Sermon on the Plain, which parallels this type of teaching. Jesus says to his disciples:

> Blessed are you who are poor, for yours is the kingdom of God. Blessed are you who are hungry now, for you will be filled. Blessed are you who weep now, for you will laugh. . .But woe to you who are rich, for you have received your consolation. Woe to you who are full now, for you will be hungry. Woe to you who are laughing now, for you will mourn and weep. Luke 6:20–26 (NRSV)

30. Hardin, *Jesus Driven Life*, 89–90.
31. Madsen, "The Rich Man and Lazarus," para. 4.

Both this parable and the Sermon on the Plain are very similar to the parable of the sheep and the goats, but none of these teach eternal torment for the wicked. There are those who will, however, face corrective punishment. I believe this much to be "clear" at least. Consistently, they are those who give the least to the poor, who tear down their fellow man to build themselves up, and who place judgement on who is righteous and who is not. However, according to Paul, even those who do this are shown mercy in spite of their disobedience (Romans 11:32).

ONE LAST WORD

There is so much rich, cultural context that simply gets lost when we pluck words out of their original intended meaning. The passages I discussed in this chapter seem to include ancient words where this happens. However, when read appropriately and without the presupposed idea that God's justice is purely retributive, the passages I discussed do not seem to argue in favor of eternal torment. Rather, I see them as powerful lessons that warn against giving into the desires of the flesh. Lessons, which if disobeyed, will bring about corrective punishment and destruction of the old self. With Jesus as my interpretive lens for how I view the Father, I cannot conclude that any of God's punishment, future or otherwise, is for anything but the purpose of correction. Thus, I find no place in Scripture where all hope is lost for the good majority or even some.

9

Conclusion

OVER THE COURSE OF this book, I have attempted to deconstruct what I believe to be many incorrect theologies—*some shared by my former self*—replacing them with an understanding of the Father who truly mirrors Jesus. As I said at the outset, for many, digesting this material is going to take a change in one's mind. Deuteronomy 6:5 tells us to "love the Lord your God with all your heart and with all your soul and with all your strength" (NIV). Jesus, in Luke 10:27, adds one's "mind" to the equation. Now that you have reached the end, having not thrown this in the garbage yet, I hope, at minimum, that you are pondering some of the same questions I used to struggle with. *Is God violent? Does God love everyone the same? Does God love me? Is he really angry with people? Does God need retribution? Sacrifice? Did Jesus save some of us from the Father?* My greater hope is that this book answered these questions and more.

In the following section, I will discuss multiple instances in which scripture mentions that every knee will bow and every tongue confess that "Jesus is Lord." But what does this really mean? In light of the context that Caesar was "lord over all" during Jesus' life, I believe this title has much larger implications than many would contend.

THE FUTURE IMPLICATIONS OF "JESUS IS LORD"

On two occasions, namely Romans 14:11 and Philippians 2:10, Paul informs us that all will acknowledge that "Jesus is Lord." Most Christians contend that all will bow and confess, but some will do so as if *defeated soldiers on a battlefield*. Thus, once God gets his acknowledgment, *then* his enemies can be cast away forever. *But is this so?*

Paul, in Philippians 2:9–11 writes: "For this reason also, God highly exalted him, and bestowed on him the name which is above every name, so that at the name of Jesus every knee will bow, of those who are in heaven and on earth and under the earth, and that every tongue will confess that Jesus Christ is Lord, to the glory of God the Father." Jesus, as Lord, is given authority to judge both the living and the dead (2 Timothy 4:1). As I discussed at length in chapter 5, the judgement of Jesus is rooted in mercy and grace—dying for us while we were yet sinners (Romans 5:8), forgiving while being murdered (Luke 23:34), and returning from the dead with the word of peace (John 20:19–23). As judge, Jesus consistently displayed perfect justice—not deeming some guilty and some innocent, but all guilty (Romans 3:23), yet all shown mercy (Romans 11:33).

If you take a look at Romans 14:11, notice that the NASB and NRSV read: "every tongue shall *give praise* [emphasis mine] to God." The Greek verb translated as "confess" or "give praise" (depending on translation) comes from the Greek verb *exomologeó*, and indeed implies not only "confession," but a giving of praise and open declaration of Jesus' lordship. In this case, Paul seems to be arguing that all will openly confess that "Jesus is Lord," giving praise all the while. Furthermore, if you take a look at the Old Testament passage in which Paul is referring (Isaiah 45:23), you will not notice any contextual evidence that suggests that God will then reject such praise. It seems the presupposed notion that God will yet cast some off into eternal darkness, even after they declare that Jesus as Lord, must be read into Romans 14:11.

Further evidence that all will confess comes from the book of Revelation. In Revelation 5, after the slain Lamb opens the book and its seven seals (5:5), the "four creatures" and elders sing the following: "Worthy are you to take the book and to break its seals, for you were slain, and purchased for God with your blood men from every tribe and tongue and people and nation. You have made them to be a kingdom and priests to our God; and they will reign upon the earth" (Revelation 5:9–10). Then, thousands of angels together say: "worthy is the Lamb that was slain to receive power and riches and wisdom and might and honor and glory and blessing" (5:12). Finally, as if in a processional, the rest: "every created thing which is in heaven and on the earth and under the earth and on the sea, and all things in them, I heard saying, 'To him who sits on the throne, and to the Lamb, be blessing and honor and glory and dominion forever and ever'" (5:13). This certainly makes one ask: What does God do with those who bow or confess "last"? Does God exact vengeance on some anyway? Was God's desire for every knee to bow to him just to prove a point, with no tangible consequence? Or, rather, does he show mercy to them in the same manner that Jesus showed mercy to his enemies? According to both Paul and the writer of the book of Revelation, all will give praise to their Lord, Jesus Christ, who, as the *Logos* of God, brought with him eschatological mercy.

THE (POTENTIAL) IMMEDIATE IMPLICATIONS OF "JESUS IS LORD"

As I mentioned in chapter 1, there are those who accuse Universalists of adhering to a doctrine that will lead to an apathetic church. However, as I demonstrated throughout chapters 4 and 5, this is simply a distracting and untrue statement. Mimetic theory teaches us that our behavior is not only determined by our imitation of others' desires, but also our imitation of the nature of whatever god we worship. Take this statement to the most extreme examples: the members of ISIS believe in an extremely violent version of Allah and thus, their behavior follows suit. (For the sake of argument, I will leave all the political reasons that also play into the development of groups like this out of my treatment here.) On the other end of the spectrum is Sufism, a more mystical understanding of Islam, where emphasis is placed on peace and equality. One of my favorite writers, Sufi mystic M.R. Bawa Muhaiyaddeen, beautifully displays his understanding of Islam in the following:

> Peace, unity, equality . . . when we are in one place, when we live in one place, eat in one place, sleep in one place, disappear in one place, die in one place, when our final judgment is given in one place, and when we finally join together *in heaven in one place* [emphasis mine], that is unity. Even when we go to that (final) place, we all live together in freedom as one family, one group. In this world and in the next world we live together in freedom, as one family of peace. This is Islam. If we find this way of peace, this is Islam.[1]

1. Muhaiyaddeen, *God's Psychology*, 181.

No matter what religion, there will be extremes of all sorts. Islam is no different. Christianity is no different. *Is Islam a religion of peace?* It depends on who you ask: a member of ISIS or Bawa Muhaiyaddeen. *Is Christianity a religion of peace?* It depends on who you ask: Jerry Falwell, George W. Bush, Mark Driscoll, and John Piper or Martin Luther King, Jr., Shane Claiborne, Leo Tolstoy, and Vernard Eller. One need not look too hard to see further examples of this everywhere.

As I demonstrated briefly in chapter 2, the violence that has been front and center in the (Constantinian) church seems to correlate to the doctrine of exclusivism and the belief in a sacrifice-demanding god. Now, what if Christians understood, as I understand it, that "Jesus is Lord" means that *all* are shown mercy? What are the immediate implications of this? What if *peace* and *forgiveness*—to the extreme Jesus took them—was practiced by, in the broadest of senses, the church? Because I believe Jesus was not talking about some "pipe-dream" when He asked his followers to pray "thy kingdom come, thy will be done on earth as it is in heaven" (Matthew 6:10—KJV), I truly believe our focus as followers of Christ is to *actually* bring this about. After all, Jesus did say "the kingdom of God is within you" (Luke 17:21) and if that is the case, are not all things possible? What if the gospel revelation *is* what I suggest it is? And what if more people knew and believed the gospel? Should that be the case, I believe real healing, real change, and a real hope for "thy kingdom come" could take hold.

In order to properly convey what I envision Jesus meant when he taught such things, I would like to use a recent life experience—one that forever changed how I viewed "community" and "the church." This was an experience that allowed me to taste the real fruits of a community of servants, where everyone else comes first and nobody defines themselves "over and above" another. What I will share seemed *like the kingdom of heaven.*

Between April 26 and May 2, 2015, I attended the "Making Peace Conference," hosted by Michael and Lorri Hardin. For an entire week, I was surrounded by a group that never once passed judgment on one another, never once seemed interested in anything other than peace and reconciliation amongst humankind, and never once made anyone feel anything but loved. Because of the shared belief in a more inclusive, gracious, and loving God; the all-inclusive love of the group seemed as radical as I understand our Lord to *actually* be.

One could say, "Well, Matthew, you were only with this group for a week!" *Fair.* However, one does not need to be with others for a certain quantity of time to experience a certain quality of relationship. The inclusive love I experienced cannot *fully* be put into words, it is only learned through experience—*tacit* knowledge.[2] That being said, I will use language anyway in an attempt to explain how I experienced the powerful healing effects of such a loving community.

Personal Healing

On May 29, 2015, *The Raven Foundation* published an essay I wrote, entitled "The Power of Positive Mimesis." I would like to quote that essay, in its entirety, as I feel it best summarizes the positive impact this group had on me.

> For those who do not know, I have a condition called "Refractory Celiac Disease." In short, it is a form of Celiac Disease that does not respond to a gluten-free diet. As an auto-immune disease, it is inflamed by stress. If anyone is not aware, I was recently (within the past few months) blackballed from my long-time church—a stressful situation to say the least. I will leave the gory details of a "flare-up" out of it—you can simply look it up on webmd.com— but all you need to know is that I have not always had the best of days. That being said, things have started looking up recently.
>
> My first article was published by *The Raven Foundation* on January 8, 2015, and it is about that time when I started pursuing my writing. Since then, I have been introduced to countless Jesus-followers and, not coincidentally, have begun to witness healing within myself I never thought possible. Just one month ago, this came to a crescendo at the "Making Peace Conference," where I was surrounded by some of the most Jesus-centered people I had ever met. It was obvious to me at that point that positive mimesis—highlighted scripturally by the command Jesus gave to "follow me"—had the power to literally change the world. Because of my introduction to so many people who have decided to take this command seriously, my world certainly has changed. *Okay, but how does this relate to medical healing? Great question!*
>
> I recently watched a "Ted Talk"[3] featuring Dr Lissa Rankin, MD, and she suggests that there is scientific proof that we can

---

2. *Tacit knowledge*: knowledge that is difficult (one could argue, impossible) to transfer to another person by means of writing it down or verbalizing it.

3. This was a talk by Dr. Rankin, entitled "Is There Scientific Proof We Can Heal Ourselves?" Found at https://www.youtube.com/watch?v=LWQfe__fNbs

have a hand in healing ourselves—and I'm not talking about the sniffles, sneezes, and aches and pains. Dr Rankin also mentions the "Spontaneous Remission Project,"[4] where case studies have been done, documenting the spontaneous remission of even stage IV cancers and AIDS. If Dr. Rankin is correct, then it certainly begs the question: Can we also heal others? Well, Professor of Medicine at Harvard Medical School, Ted Kaptchuk, believes the most essential ingredient in healing is nurturing by a "health-care provider." For both Dr Rankin and Dr Kaptchuk, practicing medicine is not about treating patients as a disease to process, but treating them with love, compassion, and positivity. Their results are pretty compelling.

Could it be that when Jesus tells us to "follow" him, he meant follow him in action, including healing? (Matthew 16:24) Is that what he meant when he said, "the one who believes in me will also do the works that I do and, in fact, will do greater works than these"? (John 14:12) *It certainly is possible . . .*

But, could simply surrounding myself with Christ-followers— imitators of Jesus—be an answer? I mean, the stress that I allowed to trigger my disease was due to an immersion into a culture whose members are all-too-often only interested in getting to the top—no matter how many they trample to get there . . . a culture that defines itself by how big, how much, how *impressive!* Every-one is self-oriented—never realizing that the self is defined by the other. This is the kingdom of men, and it has made its way into the heart and soul of American Christianity. For too long, it made its way into my own heart as well. My inability to forgive, my anger toward others, my scapegoating, was simply an imitation of those I complained about. It was a virus that kept me under its spell for too long.

I can tell you that in spite of all the negativity I was a part of, including negativity within myself, the power of a loving commu-nity, in positive imitation of Jesus, can undo what harm us humans can do. My healing started when I began practicing preemptive forgiveness. However, that didn't happen until I experienced the Christ-like love, compassion, and understanding of my new friends. I believe this type of community, taking root within the self, is "like the Kingdom of God." When Jesus-followers begin practicing the same type of forgiveness, mercy, and grace they themselves *pray for* every night, then we can start to see it on Earth as it is in heaven (Matthew 6:10).

4. The studies conducted by "Spontaneous Remission Project" can be found at http://www.noetic.org/research/project/online-spontaneous-remission-bibliography-project/

Because of the self-giving love I have recently experienced, I have not had a flare-up in over a month. Do I have the same disease I once had? Sure. However, I do not tackle this disease alone. In imitating Christ, my friends, spouse, and parents have showered me with positivity and symptoms have subsided. Is this coincidence? *Perhaps.* However, I cannot help but think that Jesus meant it when he said we will "do greater works than these," which includes healing. If our modern culture is a kingdom run by men—and it certainly is—then living amongst those who bring about the kingdom of heaven on earth will be healing of itself.

Our culture is sick and only the kingdom of God—preemptive forgiveness, non-violence, non-retribution, inclusive love—can heal such a culture. This showering of love certainly healed one of its members.

So, thank you to all those who have supported me, loved me, and continue to stand with me in the name of peace. I think we have seen enough negative mimesis—it is high time we start modeling some radical, yet positive, behavior. We have the perfect model in Jesus and I am hopeful that more will join those who have blessed me in seeing him for who he truly is. *Selah.*[5]

"On Earth as it is in Heaven"

Because I have experienced the personal healing effects of true Christian community, I cannot help but desire to share my story with others. To bring this community to the ends of the earth will require the virus I mentioned in the essay to be replaced by the power of positive mimesis—the imitation of unconditional love, mercy, grace, and forgiveness to not only those in relationship with Christ, but also to those who "do not even deserve it." Jesus said: "If you love those who love you, what reward do you have? Do not even the tax collectors do the same? If you greet only your brothers, what more are you doing than others?" (Matthew 5:46–47)

While it is easy to love the loveable, have grace on the gracious, and forgive the forgiving, how many of us *actually* love our enemies? (5:44) How many of us would walk "two miles" instead of just one with a kidnapper? (5:41) How many of us consistently pray for the members of ISIS? (5:44) As difficult as these questions are, Jesus gives us clear insight as to

---

5. Distefano, "The Power of Positive Mimesis," *in toto.*

how they should be answered. We love, bless, and offer our prayers because that is how the One we imitate behaves (5:48).

When you view everyone as loved, treating even your enemies as "brethren," odds are, you will treat them more in line with how Jesus treated his "enemies." Paul seemed to think there was no difference between himself and his unbelieving Jewish brothers and sisters when he writes: "I have great sorrow and unceasing anguish in my heart. For I could wish that I myself were accursed and cut off from Christ for the sake of my own people, my kindred according to the flesh" (Romans 9:2–3). This begs the question: *Who are Paul's own "people"?* If you stick to the tradition of Calvin, it would be the "elect" (Romans 9:23). However, as I mentioned in chapter 7, Paul concludes his thoughts regarding the "elect" in Romans 11, when he writes:

> Just as you were once disobedient to God but have now received mercy because of their disobedience, so they have now been disobedient in order that, by the mercy shown to you, they too may now receive mercy. For God has imprisoned all in disobedience so that he may be merciful to all (. . .) for from him and through him and to him are all things. (Romans 11:30–31; 36—NRSV)

It seems that, according to Paul, we are all in this together—all complicit and deserving "wrath" (at some point) because of our disobedience, yet all shown mercy in spite of it.

If we truly see ourselves, not as individuals, but as *interdividuals*, as René Girard suggests, then we can begin to see where Paul is coming from. Honestly, what is the difference if I am cut off from Christ or if one of my own brothers or sisters is? If we are truly "one body in Christ," then to lose one member of the body is akin to losing one's self. This seems to include our enemies—those still disobedient and deserving wrath.

If we take this stance—that all are a part of Christ's flock—it makes the trying times a bit more palatable, as I see it. Furthermore, if we "have died with Christ,"[6] we have nothing to hold us back from treating all, even those who insist on becoming our violent *enemy*, as "made in the image and likeness of God." Jesus becomes our foundation for forgiveness in John 20:23, when he tells us "if you forgive the sins of any, their sins have been forgiven." This ability to forgive at all times is what sets us free—free from our mimetic entanglement which we so often find ourselves in. And as I discussed in chapter 5, the resurrection is the promise that even if we follow Jesus unto death, the Father will make us alive again.

6. See Romans 6:1–11.

As I mentioned in the essay above, when the radical forgiveness of Jesus becomes central in belief and practice, the world will begin to look like the kingdom of God. But, Christianity has to begin to buy in. She must stop focusing so much attention on the "next life," and focus instead on the here and now—on earth *now* as it is in heaven. The church seems to be living under the mantra of "our home is not of this world." While I wholeheartedly agree with that phrase, I do not agree with the intent, or the escapist mentality it is interpreted with. Many long for the rapture— "pre-trib" preferably[7]—when Jesus can snatch them out of this world that is destined for utter destruction. What I believe is a better interpretation and mindset, is that we long for a day when the chariots, horses, and bows of war are cut off,[8] when swords are beaten into plowshares,[9] and when peace reigns forever. *That is home!* This home we long for is founded upon perfect peace, forgiveness, and love. We do not have to wait for the afterlife to create an existence that is "like the kingdom of heaven." We can begin to create a piece of heaven now by scraping our tanks, drones, and AR-15s, by beating our handguns into plowshares, by disarming nuclear bombs, and by seeing Jesus in the "least of these."

LIFE WITHOUT FEAR

Ah, to live life without fear! So many live under the freedom-crippling doctrine of eternal conscious torment, which *is* a doctrine of fear. Many take no issue with this, claiming the fear of God is a good thing. Throughout many of the psalms and proverbs primarily, but also littered throughout the Hebrew Scriptures, fearing God is must.

- *"The fear of the Lord is the beginning of knowledge"* Proverbs 1:7—NIV
- *"You shall not wrong one another, but you shall fear your God."* Leviticus 25:17
- *"You shall fear only the Lord your God."* Deuteronomy 6:13
- *"The fear of the Lord is clean, enduring forever."* Psalm 19:9

As Lord and righteous judge (2 Timothy 4:8), Jesus carries the keys to the kingdom of God (2 Timothy 4:1)—which extends from "sea to sea . . . to the

---

7. Scripture in support of a pre-tribulation rapture are as follows:

8. See Zechariah 9:10.

9. See Isaiah 2:4.

ends of the earth" (Zechariah 9:10). And yet, Jesus as the revealed image of the Father constantly tells his followers to "fear not."

When Jesus tells us to not be afraid, it is because, as I have referenced on numerous occasions, God is love (1 John 4:8) and "perfect love casts out fear" (1 John 4:18). Before the full revelation of God was seen in Jesus, "the fear of the Lord" was the beginning of wisdom and knowledge. After Jesus, the Word of God is revealed fully and fear can be properly cast out. And when that perfect love of God is embraced, all fear subsides. The fear of death, of punishment, of a retributive god—all cast out by the perfect love of the true God. The Father is perfect love and as such, gives freely. Michael Hardin writes:

> When Paul in 2 Corinthians 3:6 and the writer to the Hebrews (chapters 8 and 10) speak of the New Covenant, the covenant inaugurated on the last night of Jesus' life, they both understand that obedience is not compelled, coerced, or compulsory. Obedience as love is the willingness to offer oneself to God as God has offered God's self to us.[10]

When all eventually bow their knees and confess that "Jesus is Lord," it will not be because of fear, but because of "obedience as love"—an apocalypse "within us," as Paul puts it in Galatians 1:15–17.[11]

Paul's internal apocalypse transformed a violent persecutor into arguably the church's greatest apostle—her greatest saint. This transformation was not due to some fear of threat of death or worse, hell. (Paul himself said, in Romans 7:11 that he had already died.) Rather, it was due in whole to the revelation of who Jesus was: the revealer of God, who is love and light, who is merciful, gracious, and compassionate—in a word, overwhelming.

Our Loved Ones

> If I truly love my own daughter, for example, and love her even as I love myself, then I simply cannot be happy knowing that she is suffering or that she is otherwise miserable—unless, of course, I can somehow believe that, in the end, all will be well for her. But if I cannot believe this, if I were to believe instead that she has been

---

10. Hardin, *The Jesus Driven Life*, 35

11. In Galatians 1:16, Paul writes: "*apokalypsai ton Huion autou en emoi,*" or "apocalypsed/revealed the Son in me." In other words, the Son is revealed *in* Paul, not *outside of* Paul.

lost to me forever—even if I were to believe that, by her own will, she has made herself intolerably evil—my own happiness could never be complete, not so long as I continued to love her and to yearn for her redemption. For I would always know what could have been, and I would always experience that as a terrible tragedy and an unacceptable loss, one for which no compensation is even conceivable.[12]

As I mentioned early on, the thought of any of my loved ones burning forever in eternal torment literally caused me grief throughout my younger years. This horror manifested most intensely when, in my early teen years, my good friend Ryan was killed in an auto accident when he was thrown from the bed of a pick-up truck. I remember lying awake at night trying to conceptualize the fact that because Ryan was not a Christian, he would be tortured for a billion years, multiplied by a billion more; and since that does not even cover it I will stop there—we all understand infinite cannot be added to, subtracted from, multiplied with anything, nor divided. How was I ever going to enjoy Heaven knowing that Ryan was not going to be there? Moreover, how about my non-practicing Roman Catholic grandmother who was like a second mother for me? Does her death potentially thwart God's desire to save her or did he never desire that in the first place? None of the traditional answers worked for me:

. . . *You never know what happens on someone's death bed* . . .

. . . *There are mysteries we will never know* . . .

. . . *God will make it right in the end* . . .

And even if those kind of statements comfort some, they certainly do not answer the bigger "truth" that countless mothers and daughters, fathers and sons, brothers and sisters, husbands and wives, and all sorts of loved-ones will be torn and ripped apart forever, in a system that certainly did not have to be set up like Western Christianity attests it is. How does one reconcile this? How is this not a doctrine of fear?

With the doctrine of universal reconciliation something I now hold to, I no longer fear that my loved ones will spend eternity in hell. I no longer fear that *any potential* separation from my daughter will ever be eternal. Talbott explains it as follows:

We will no longer fear, for example that our Creator might permit an honest mistake in theology to jeopardize our future. We will

12. Talbott, *Inescapable Love of God*, 126–27.

simply proceed in the confidence that he knows us from the inside out far better than we know ourselves, that he will appreciate the ambiguities, the confusions, and the perplexities we face far better than we do; and that he will understand the historical and cultural factors that shape our beliefs far better than any historian does. Such a Creator—loving, intimate, and wise—would know how to work with us in infinitely complex ways, how to shatter our illusions and transform our thinking when necessary, and how best to reveal to us in the end.[13]

My hope is that our Creator, wise and loving as he is, would not be a god who tortures, allows the torture, or obliterates something made in his image and likeness. That is the Janus-faced god, the two-faced deity who seems to be a reflection of mankind.

Similar to how all humans are made in the image and likeness of God, so too are children made in their parents' image and likeness. Scripture gives us this analogy of God as Father over and over again. Whatever happens to one's child may as well happen to the parent. If all are not reconciled—if parents lose their children forever (or vice-versa) how can the writer of Revelation state the following?

"And He will wipe away every tear from their eyes; and there will no longer be any death; there will no longer be any mourning, or crying, or pain; the first things have passed away." Revelation 21:4

With love as a foundation, I only see this happening if all things are reconciled in the end. Short of that, any Heaven I could obtain apart from my daughter would have to be due to a hardening of my heart toward her or ignorance of her existence. Do these options sound loving? My hope is that the gospel is the good news I believe it is; one that graciously extends to my loved ones who, if we are to take a Christ-like or Pauline approach, would include everyone.

CONCLUDING REMARKS

A Quick Look Back

As I mentioned on a few occasions, Christians too often carry presuppositions into their theology. Jesus is met with a preconceived understanding about God; his story read in light of preexisting Hebrew Scripture. Concepts

13. Talbott, *Concerning False Prophets*, 10.

like justice and vengeance are understood prior to witnessing how Jesus himself understood these ideas. Hermeneutics are established prior to asking, "How did Jesus read Scripture?" Hell, at least amongst the circles I grew up in, was always interpreted as eternal torment without understanding how to properly interpret Gehenna in the context of Second Temple Judaism, the context of a non-retributive eschatology, or frankly, the context of anything other than American Protestanism. The church is long overdue for a deconstruction of many of her presuppositions.

Mimetic theory, introduced in chapter 4, offers a compelling explanation as to why many of these presuppositions about God arise in the first place. Throughout the ages, mankind has projected countless incorrect ideas about who God is. This is also why many of the gods throughout history have been retributive—demanding sacrifice in one way or another. Because of the work of René Girard, we can now see that desire for sacrifice is a man-made notion—a projection onto God that is simply not an attribute he possesses.

Mimetic theory also gives us a fresh lens with which to view human religion and culture, and thus, a fresh lens with which to reconstruct a better theology. In light of the Gospel, theology can begin where it needs to—at the cross. It is this place, Calvary, where for the first time there is a standard by which to measure all claims about God. There is a model with which to judge whether something is "of God," or "of human origin." This revelation forever changes how we should view the atonement (chapter 5), hermeneutics (chapter 6), the apostle Paul (chapter 7), and eschatological punishment (chapter 8). This model is Jesus Christ.

Jesus: The Beginning and End . . . and Everything in Between!

In the beginning was the Word, and the Word was with God, and the Word was God. He was in the beginning with God. All things came into being through him, and without him not one thing came into being. What has come into being in him was life, and the life was the light of all people. The light shines in the darkness, and the darkness did not overcome it. John 1:1–5

As Christians, everything we do should be Jesus-centered. Our way of interpreting Scripture, our interpersonal relationships, our marriages and child-rearing, our political associations—all viewed through the lens of "following Jesus." Sadly, this is not the case with many who bear the title

"Christian," and the church has suffered. To reverse this—in order to restore things—everything must begin and end with Christ.

The Jesus I have come to know came to serve all, becoming our model so that we may mirror him in desiring to love as his Father loves. The Jesus I have fallen madly in love with never showed favoritism of one group over another and never gave the ultimatum, "Follow me, or else!" In fact, witness how Jesus famously encounters an adultress who is about to be stoned by the religious authorities. John 8:3–11 read:

> The scribes and the Pharisees brought a woman who had been caught in adultery; and making her stand before all of them, they said to him, 'Teacher, this woman was caught in the very act of committing adultery. Now in the law Moses commanded us to stone such women. Now what do you say?' They said this to test him, so that they might have some charge to bring against him. Jesus bent down and wrote with his finger on the ground. When they kept on questioning him, he straightened up and said to them, 'Let anyone among you who is without sin be the first to throw a stone at her.' And once again he bent down and wrote on the ground. When they heard it, they went away, one by one, beginning with the elders; and Jesus was left alone with the woman standing before him. Jesus straightened up and said to her, 'Woman, where are they? Has no one condemned you?' She said, 'No one, sir.' And Jesus said, 'Neither do I condemn you. Go your way, and from now on do not sin again.' NRSV

Notice how Jesus does not rake the woman over the coals before he sends her on her way. He does not say, "Now believe in me so you can be 'saved.'" He simply offers mercy and commands her to cease sinning. Even though he was the only one there who was indeed without sin and thus, could condemn her, he does not. Remember, Jesus came not to judge, but to save (John 3:17).[14]

When we claim to be followers of Jesus, we enter into a new way of being—a transformation from everything we once knew. The forgiveness Jesus displayed on the cross is the perfect manifestation of the love the Father has for all of humanity. Thus, it is the model for how we are to manifest that same love to others. The Holy Spirit Jesus breathed out at Pentecost lives within us and gives us the boldness to speak the words of forgiveness—to be peacemakers through and through.

---

14. Many then read John 3:18–19 with a presupposed view of "judgment" as retributive, which leads to an exclusivist theology and thus, an exclusivist reading of John 3.

"Father, forgive them; for they know not what they are doing."
"Father, forgive them; for they know not what they are doing."
"Father, forgive them; for they know not what they are doing."

This phrase was uttered over and over by Jesus while he hung on that Roman cross. This was his mantra, even unto death. It was also his mantra after death, when he came to his disciples with the same message, the message of peace. He cannot help but love us dearly. He cannot help but offer forgiveness to all of us because we have no clue what we are doing. When Jesus is handed over to our satanic powers and principalities, he conquers them all like a lamb, as if slain.[15] And because of this, he is given the name above all names and as Lord, he will rule forevermore.

The Father's mercy endures forever.
The gates of New Jerusalem never shut.
The "hound of heaven" never tires.

Christ's love conquers all.

---

15. See Revelation 5:6.

Appendix

Deliver Us from Evil
Jesus, Satan, and the Holy Spirit

by Adam Ericksen

IF YOU ARE LIKE me, you have come to the end of Matthew's book filled with awe, gratitude, and a renewed sense of mission. Matthew has done us a great service by documenting an ancient and traditional strand within Christianity of universal salvation. Indeed, Matthew has shown that evil, hell, and corruption do not have the last word—God does.

All Set Free has invited us on an exciting mission of good news. I agree with Matthew when he states: *"If God can find a way to reconcile with all who have sinned against him, so too can I do that in my own life."* The world needs more people to participate in the divine life of God. As Paul states in 1 Corinthians 5:19 that divine life is: "reconciling the world to himself, not counting their trespasses against them, and entrusting the message of reconciliation to us."

If we are honest, we will admit that we often become distracted from the divine life of reconciliation. And so Matthew has asked me to briefly explore with you the mechanism that distracts Christians from participating in the divine life. That distraction is named satan. But I refuse to give satan the last word to such a wonderful book as this. So I will end this epilogue with a meditation on the Holy Spirit.

SATAN: THE ACCUSER

The first time satan is developed in the Old Testament is in the book of Job. Whenever the word "satan" is used in the Old Testament, it refers to a title, not a proper name. For example, in Job, the word satan is accompanied by the definitive article "the." This indicates that that "the satan" is not an actual being, but a job title or a verb.

In English, we would translate the Hebrew word "satan" into *accuser.* Curiously in Job, the satan is on God's team. The satan works for God as part of the divine council. Its role is to be like God's prosecuting attorney, roaming the earth, accusing people of sinning against God.

The satan is the accuser but we should not overly spiritualize it. René Girard has taught us that satan is not primarily a red figure with horns and a pitch fork. That is a mythology that gives satan too big a role and far too much credit. It allows us to conveniently blame satan for our own responsibility in participating in the satan. "Satan made me do it!" No, if we want to know what the satan is truly like, we do not need to look to a mythical being; we must simply look to ourselves.

In his book *Job: The Victim of His People*, Girard claims that the satanic principle of accusation is a human phenomenon. Whenever we point the finger of accusation against another, we have become the satan.

Interestingly, after the second chapter of Job, the satan figure fades away, never to be heard from again. For the next thirty-nine chapters, Job downplays the satan in order to emphasize the human tendency to participate in satanic accusations. Job suffered the loss of his livelihood, his house, and the death of his children. To make matters worse, Job has four "friends," who are a good example of what to do, and what not to do, in the face of suffering. At one point, Job's anguish was so bad, and his physical shape so broken, that his friends did not recognize him at first. As they came closer to Job, "They raised their voices and wept aloud; they tore their robes and threw dust in the air upon their heads. They sat with him on the ground seven days and seven nights, and no one spoke a word to him, for they saw that his suffering was very great."[1]

We often want to know what to say in the face of such tragic suffering, but usually words just get in the way. The friends practice what pastoral theologians call the "ministry of presence" where you do not need to have the right words to say in the face of suffering. In the midst of immense

---

1. Job 2:12–13.

misery, showing up, weeping out loud, and sitting together in silence is often the best way to practice the divine life of reconciliation.

Job soon laments his situation and his friends become uncomfortable with his pain. They want to provide answers and their answers come in the form of satanic accusations. Paradoxically, those satanic accusations that serve as answers are based on religious conviction.

Certainly, each friend claims, Job *must* have done something wrong. He must have sinned against God to deserve such punishment. The "friends" unite in accusations against Job. In seeking to find answers to Job's suffering, they fall into the scapegoating mechanism of casting blame. They have fallen into the satanic mechanism of accusation.

The satanic mechanism of accusation functions as a model for humanity. It invites us into a way of life that distortedly mirrors the divine life of reconciliation. For the satan offers a way towards reconciliation, but that reconciliation comes at the expense of a scapegoat.

Yet the friends firmly believe that they are on God's side. They think they are righteous and that Job is a sinner. Job's friends reveal that identity of "goodness" can indeed be a very dangerous thing, especially when wielded by religious people. As mimetic beings, we gain our identity in relationship with others. When we scapegoat others by accusing them of being bad, we sense that we are good.

When we form an identity of goodness over against another whom we label evil, we participate in the satanic mechanism of accusation. That is a distorted sense of identity that James Alison calls a fake goodness.[2]

Job, however, does not take the bait. In the face of satanic accusations levied against him, Job maintains his innocence. He does not claim to be sinless, but does contend that he does not deserve the suffering inflicted upon him. Job's claim to relative innocence is remarkable. As mimetic beings, when the crowd unites against us we can easily start to believe in the crowd's accusations.

In the end, God declares that Job was right and his friends were wrong. God says to the friends, "You have not spoken of me what is right, as my servant Job has." (Job 42:7) Job was right to maintain his innocence and his friends were wrong to accuse him.

Many people have a spiritual practice of identifying with characters in the Bible. For a long time, I identified with Job. My mother died when I was twenty-one. Job's endurance of faith and ability to question religious

2. Alison, *Jesus the Forgiving Victim*, 474.

laws that blame the victim became a model of faith for me at a time when I needed it most.

Since that personal tragedy, I've had spiritual mentors who have challenged me to identify with other characters of the Bible. I had my Job moment, but I have had many more moments when I have acted like his friends. Far more than I would like to admit, I am just like Job's friends. I have a tendency to split the world up into good and evil. Of course, I am on the side of good. And like Job's friends, my identity as good over against another as evil is based on self-deception and satanic accusations. When I identify with Job's friends, I start to become more self-critical and more honest about my tendency to follow in the footsteps of the satan's accusations.

JESUS, SATAN, AND EVIL

In the New Testament the satan is no longer a member of God's divine council. The figure Satan develops a slightly larger persona, but still rarely appears in the account. Satan's role is still the accuser, but similarly with Job, satan's role is downplayed in favor of emphasizing the human propensity to accuse and scapegoat our fellow human beings.

During his baptism, Jesus received confirmation of what had already been eternally true—that he was God's son. Then the Spirit led him into the desert where he was tempted by the devil. The devil's temptation came in the form of an implicit accusation that God was wrong about Jesus' divine Sonship. The devil tempted Jesus to prove himself with this suggestion: "*If* you are the Son of God, command these stones to become loaves of bread." (Matthew 4:3—emphasis mine)

If: such a small word but so full of significance. Jesus had just received his identity from God. He is the Son of God. Like the serpent tempted Adam and Eve to doubt God's loving relationship with them, so too did the devil tempt Jesus into doubting God's loving relationship with him. Satan tempts Jesus by suggesting that he needs to prove his relationship with God. Satan's implicit accusation is that God is not as good as God says he is. In making this accusation, satan attempts to act as a model for Jesus. He seduces Jesus with seemingly good things—food, safety, and power. Satan says to Jesus: "All these I will give to you, if you will fall down and worship me." (4:9)

I assume that, in all of his humanity, Jesus was profoundly tempted to worship the devil. We all want food, safety, and power. But satan's offer came at a price. At this critical moment in his ministry, indeed, in human history, Jesus could have sold his soul to the devil—the Tempter, the Accuser. To worship the devil would have been to take the devil on as his model. Jesus could have produced enough food for everyone by turning stone into bread, he could have created safety so that even if you jumped from high buildings and fell to the earth you would not be hurt, and he could have ruled all the kingdoms of the world. But he would have accomplished those things by following satan. He would have provided for the many by eventually accusing and scapegoating the few.

Jesus was tempted in every way, but he refused to take satan on as a model. Rather, he would continue to receive his identity from his Father. Jesus revealed that there is no "satan" within God. As Matthew has taught us throughout this book, God is not a Janus-faced mixture of good and evil. God has nothing to do with the satanic mechanism of accusation. As 1 John tells us: "God is light and in him there is no darkness at all."[3]

Jesus finally revealed God's universal love for humanity. He allows us to trust that God loves us just as we are and that any other message is not from God. Rather, it originates from the satanic principle of accusation.

In revealing God's universal love, he confronted the human scapegoating mechanism. Jesus claimed that the devil "was a murderer from the beginning."[4] Satan—the devil—led Cain to kill his brother Abel. And Satan has been leading us to kill one another ever since.

God's will for Jesus was not to take the Father's holy wrath upon himself. Jesus reveals that the Father has no wrath. Any doctrine that claims God's wrath was diverted onto Jesus while he hung on the cross is not from God. Rather, it too originates from the satanic principle of accusation.

Jesus absorbed human satanic violence that united the crowd, religious elite, and political rulers against him. In return for that violence, Jesus offered us a way out through divine forgiveness. On the cross, Jesus was sent to hell by his fellow human beings. It is humans who send one another to hell, not God. Hell is our responsibility, not God's. Jesus went to hell so that our pattern of sending one another to hell would be transformed—so that we would stop scapegoating one another and instead, we would love one another as God has loved us.[5]

3. 1 John 1:5.
4. John 8:44.
5. John 13:34.

DELIVER US FROM EVIL

The good news is that we do not have to defeat satan or evil. Nor do we have to save the world. That is not our burden to bear. Jesus has already done those things. In fact, Jesus gives us specific instructions for how to manage evil in the world. He taught us that evil is something that we are to be delivered from.

Because we are mimetic, we absorb our environment. Evil is infectious. When we battle against evil, it begins to consume us. We become the very evil we battle against. Nietzsche was not Girard's favorite philosopher, but he was right about this: "He who fights with monsters should look to it that he himself does not become a monster. And when you gaze long into an abyss the abyss also gazes into you."[6]

When we stare into the abyss of evil, it stares directly back and infects us. When we fight violently with monsters, we become the very monster we fight against. Girard calls this mimetic doubling. And Jesus calls us away from becoming the evil we fight against, which is why he taught us to pray that the Father would "deliver us from evil."[7] For Christians, evil is that which we are constantly being delivered from. Unfortunately, Christians tend to be like Job's friends who found themselves caught up in the satanic mechanism of accusation. Christians tend to be like Jesus' disciples who betrayed, abandoned, and denied him during his time of need. Christians tend to be like Paul who, before his conversion, breathed threats of murder against his scapegoats. Christians tend to be like Adam and Eve, who continually eat the forbidden fruit and believe we are the judges of good and evil in the world.

But Christians are more than that. Christians are forgiven scapegoaters who repeatedly find ourselves repenting from the satanic mechanism. In other words, Jesus taught us to pray for deliverance from evil because he knew our propensity to be consumed by evil.

Fighting evil with evil has the added misfortune of stifling our imaginations for the good. Fighting violence with violence is not creative. It only assures us a future of destruction at our own violent hands.

Fortunately, our future is not doomed to an apocalyptic destruction of our own making. We have a choice. We can drop our weapons. We can stop satanically accusing one another. We can receive God's love for us and share

---

6. Nietzsche, *Beyond Good and Evil*, Aphorism 146.

7. Matthew 6:13.

that love with others, including those we call our enemies. But even more important than the choices we make, we have the Holy Spirit.

THE HOLY SPIRIT: THE DEFENSE ATTORNEY

In the Gospel of John, Jesus calls the Holy Spirit the *Paraclete*. It is composed of two Greek words that mean "beside" and "to call out." Girard makes the point that: "The principal meaning of *parakletos* is 'lawyer for the defense,' 'defender of the accused.' The term *paraclete* referred to a defense attorney in an ancient courtroom."[8]

If satan tempts us to make accusations against our scapegoats, the Holy Spirit leads us to stand with those very same scapegoats. It is important to note that guilt or innocence does not matter to the satanic mechanism—all that matters is that satan gives us a sense of righteous goodness over and against our enemies.

Jesus was not only one with the Father; he was also one with the Holy Spirit who led him to stand with the scapegoats of his culture. The satanic life is one that makes accusations. The divine life is one that leads us to love our enemies—our cultural scapegoats—just as God loves us.

The Holy Spirit guides us into participating in the divine life by creatively standing with cultural scapegoats. As we receive God's forgiveness, we are able to offer forgiveness to others. In doing so, we find ourselves being delivered from evil. We resist the temptation to scapegoat anyone, including those we label as guilty scapegoaters. Instead, the Holy Spirit emboldens us for an exciting and creative future as we walk with Jesus, healing ourselves and the world from the satanic mechanism of accusation through God's universal and eternal love.

BIBLIOGRAPHY

Allison, James. *Jesus the Forgiving Victim*. Glenview: DOERS, 2013.
Girard, René. *I See Satan Fall Like Lightning*. Translated by James G. Williams. New York: Orbis, 2001.
———. *Job: The Victim of His People*. Stanford: Stanford University Press, 1987.
Nietzsche, Friedrich. *Beyond Good and Evil*. Leipzig: 1886.

8. Girard, *I See Satan*, 190.

Bibliography

Allen, Ken. "What is 'Christian Universalism'?" http://www.auburn.edu/~allenkc/chr-univ.html.

Alison, James. *Knowing Jesus*. Springfield: Templegate, 1994.

Andrade, Gabriel. "Rene Girard (1923-)" In *Internet Encyclopedia of Philosophy*. http://www.iep.utm.edu/girard/.

Augustine. *Confessions and Enchiridion*. Translated and edited by Albert C. Outler. Philadelphia: Westminster Press, 1955.

————. *De Correctione Donatistarum 22*. Translated and edited by Philip Schaff. A Select Library of the Nicene and Post-Nicene Fathers. Buffalo: Christian Literature, 1887. http://www.thomastalbott.com/terror.php.

Barclay, William. *William Barclay: A Spiritual Autobiography*. Grand Rapids: Eerdmans, 1977.

Blevins, Jordan. "A Relational God of Peace." Lancaster: Preaching Peace. http://www.preachingpeace.org/images/Relational_God_of_Peace_-_Book_of_Peace_Conference.pdf.

Borg, Marcus. *Jesus: A New Vision: Spirit, Culture, and the Life of Discipleship*. San Francisco: HarperOne, 1991.

Distefano, Matthew. "The Power of Positive Mimesis." The Raven Foundation, 2015. https://www.ravenfoundation.org/the-power-of-positive-mimesis/.

Ebenezer, Irpeel. *Understanding the Gift of Salvation: And a Concise History of How the Church through Ignorance And Unbelief Lost the Power of the Holy Spirit*. Bloomington: AuthorHouse, 2012.

Enns, Peter. "Jesus didn't read his Bible like we do—(from The Bible Tells Me So)." http://www.patheos.com/blogs/peterenns/2014/09/jesus-and-his-bible-from-the-bible-tells-me-so/.

————. *The Bible Tells Me So: Why Defending Scripture Has Made Us Unable to Read It*. New York: HarperOne, 2014.

Flood, Derek. *Disarming Scripture: Cherry-picking Liberals, Violence-loving Conservatives, and Why We All Need to learn to Read the Bible like Jesus Did*. San Francisco: Metanoia, 2014.

Gier, Nicholas F. "Hebrew Henotheism." http://www.webpages.uidaho.edu/ngier/henotheism.htm.

Girard, René. *The Girard Reader*. Edited by James G. Williams. New York: Crossroad Herder, 1996.

Bibliography

————. *I See Satan Fall Like Lightning*. Translated by James G. Williams. New York: Orbis, 2001.

————. *Things Hidden Since the Foundation of the World*. Translated by Stephen Bann and Michael Metteer. Stanford: Stanford University Press, 1987.

Hamerton-Kelly, Robert, ed. *Violent Origins: Ritual Killing and Cultural Foundation*. Stanford: Stanford University Press, 1987.

Hanson, J.W. *The Bible Hell*. Boston: Universalist, 1888. http://www.tentmaker.org/books/ TheBibleHell.html.

————. *The Greek Word Aion—Aionios, Translated Everlasting—Eternal in the Holy Bible, Shown to Denote Limited Duration*. Chicago: Northwestern Universalist, 1875. http://www.tentmaker.org/books/Aion_lim.html.

————. *Universalism: The Prevailing Doctrine of the Christian Church During Its First Five Hundred years*. Boston and Chicago: Universalist, 1899. http://www.tentmaker.org/ books/Prevailing.html.

Hardin, Michael. "The God of Pat Robertson." Lancaster: Preaching Peace, 2008. http:// www.preachingpeace.org/images/The_God_of_Pat_Robertson.pdf.

————. "Guest Q & R with Michael Hardin: 'The wrath of God stuff bothers me . . .'" http://brianmclaren.net/archives/blog/guest-q-r-with-michael-hardin-th.html.

————. *The Jesus Driven Life: Reconnecting Humanity with Jesus*. Lancaster: JDL, 2012.

————. "Must God be Violent?: A Diagnosis and Prescription for Modern Christianity." Lancaster: Preaching Peace, 2013. http://www.preachingpeace.org/26-articles-ebooks/articles-ebooks-by-michael-hardin/94-must-god-be-violent-a-diagnosis-prescription-for-modern-christianity.html.

————. "Reading the Bible from a Peacemaking Perspective." Lancaster: Preaching Peace, 2012. http://www.preachingpeace.org/teaching-resources/articles/26-articles-ebooks/articles-ebooks-by-michael-hardin/79-the-satan-free-e-book.html.

————. "Romans 5:12–21: An Exegesis by Michael Hardin." Lancaster: Preaching Peace, 2015.

————. *The Satan*. Lancaster: Preaching Peace, 2013. http://www.preachingpeace. org/teaching-resources/articles/26-articles-ebooks/articles-ebooks-by-michael-hardin/79-the-satan-free-e-book.html.

————. "The Pillars of Culture: Prohibition, Ritual and Myth." Lancaster: Preaching Peace. http://www.preachingpeace.org/teaching-resources/articles/23-articles-ebooks/introductory-articles/55-the-pillars-of-culture-prohibition-ritual-and-myth.html.

————. "The Scapegoat." Lancaster: Preaching Peace. http://www.preachingpeace.org/ news/23-articles-ebooks/introductory-articles/56-the-scapegoat.html.

Heim, Mark. *Saved from Sacrifice: A Theology of the Cross*. Grand Rapids: Eerdmans, 2006.

Heiser, Michael S. "Deuteronomy 32:8 and the Sons of God." http://www.thedivinecouncil. com/DT32BibSac.pdf.

Holy, Ravi. "Damned Nonsense: An Argument for Universalism." BA Hons. Diss., University of Bristol, Trinity College, 2005.

Jackson, Wayne. "Will Everyone Go to Heaven?" https://www.christiancourier.com/ articles/741-will-everyone-go-to-heaven.

Jersak, Bradley. *Her Gates Will Never Be Shut: Hope, Hell, and the New Jerusalem*. Eugene: Wipf & Stock, 2010.

Jones, Steve. "Calvinism Critiqued by a Former Calvinist." http://www.auburn. edu/~allenkc/openhse/calvinism.html.

Josephus, Flavius. *The Wars of the Jews.* Translated by William Whiston. Project Gutenberg. Salt Lake City: Project Gutenberg, 2009.

Ludlow, Morwenna. "Universalism in the History of Christianity." In *Universal Salvation?: The Current Debate,* edited by Robin Parry and Christopher Partridge. Grand Rapids: Eerdmans, 2003.

Lewis, C.S. *The Problem of Pain.* New York: HarperOne, 2001.

Luther, Martin. *The Heidelberg Disputation.* The Book of Concord. http://www. bookofconcord.org/heidelberg.php.

Machuga, Ric. *Three Theological Mistakes: How to Correct Enlightenment Assumptions about God, Miracles, and Free Will.* Eugene: Cascade, 2015.

Madsen, Kacy. "The Rich Man and Lazarus." http://wesley.nnu.edu/fileadmin/imported_ site/biblical_studies/parables/ma-lk16_19–31.htm.

McDonald, Brian. "Violence and the Lamb Slain: An Interview with Rene Girard." *Touchstone: A Journal of Mere Christianity* 16, no. 10 (2003). http://www. touchstonemag.com/archives/article.php?id=16–10-040-i.

Meltzoff, Andrew N,, and Wolfgang Prinz, eds. *The Imitative Mind: Development, Evolution, and Brain Bases.* Cambridge: Cambridge University Press, 2002.

Moltmann, Jürgen. *The Coming of God: Christian Eschatology.* Minneapolis: Augsburg Fortress, 2004.

———. *The Trinity and the Kingdom.* Minneapolis: Fortress, 1993.

Muhaiyaddeen, Bawa. *God's Psychology: A Sufi Explanation.* Philadelphia: Fellowship, 2007.

Oughourlian, Jean-Michel. *The Puppet of Desire: The Psychology of Hysteria, Possession, and Hypnosis.* Translated by Eugene Webb. Stanford: Stanford University Press, 2001.

Plato. *Protagoras.* Edited by Gregory Vlastos. Translated by Benjamin Jowett and Martin Oswald. New York: Bobbs-Merrill, 1956.

Parker, T.H.L. *John Calvin: A Biography.* Philadelphia: Westminster John Knox Press, 2007.

Rabé, Andre. *Desire Found Me.* Andre Rabe: 2015.

Reitan, Eric. "Human Freedom and the Impossibility of Eternal Damnation." In *Universal Salvation?: The Current Debate,* edited by Robin Parry and Christopher Partridge. Grand Rapids: Eerdmans, 2003.

Sproul, R.C. *Saved from What?* Wheaton: Crossway, 2002.

Stetson, Eric. "The History of Universalism." http://www.christianuniversalist.org/ resources/articles/history-of-universalism/.

Swartley, Willard M. *Covenant of Peace: The Missing Peace in New Testament Theology and Ethics.* Grand Rapids: Eerdmans, 2006.

Talbott, Thomas. *The Inescapable Love of God.* Second ed. Eugene: Cascade, 2014.

———. "Concerning False Prophets and the Abuse of Revelation." http://www.willamette. edu/~ttalbott/FALSE_PROPHETS.PDF.

———. "Toward a Better Understanding of Universalism." In *Universal Salvation?: The Current Debate,* edited by Robin Parry and Christopher Partridge. Grand Rapids: Eerdmans, 2003.

Made in the USA
San Bernardino, CA
23 February 2020